Copyrighted Material

CLEP® Introductory Psychology

Gotham City Ventures, LLC
500 Westover Dr. #6479
Sanford, NC 27330
http://www.gothamcityventures.com/

ISBN: 978-0-9964591-2-9
Copyright ©2016 by Gotham City Publishing
All rights reserved. None of the material found in this study guide may be reproduced without permission from the publisher.
Printed in the USA

Disclaimer/Liability Release:
The publication of this book is for the purpose of examination preparation. Gotham City Ventures does not guarantee the accuracy and completeness of the information contained herein and cannot claim liability in relation to the information or opinions contained within this study guide. Gotham city ventures will not be held liable for damages of any kind related to the materials found in this study guide.

Steps to Achieving Success!

Step 1- Test Taking/Study Skills Review
Gain knowledge in test taking and study skills with over 25 pages of review! Increase your chances of passing the exam by determining your learning style, how to study well and strategies for approaching exam questions.

Step 2- Complete Content Review
Focus on the exam content with a comprehensive review. CreditPREP provides you with a well written and organized presentation of content within this manual and access to online, mobile friendly flashcards. These flashcards allow you to take advantage of every spare moment in your hectic life! Please utilize this valuable resource with the instructions below:

> **FLASHCARD ACCESS:**
> Please go to www.gothamcitypublishing.com
> Click on CreditPREP Flashcards Registration
> Follow the Directions Provided to Access the Flashcards

Step 3- Test Your Knowledge
Use the full length practice exam provided at the end of this manual to determine your knowledge of Developmental Psychology. Use the results of this exam to efficiently focus your final studying efforts.

Step 4- Take Your Exam
Apply the credits earned toward your college degree and future career!!

Table of Contents

Preparing for Your Exam 6
- Study Skills 6
- Scheduling Your Test 11
- Last Minute Preparation for Testing 12

Test-Taking Tips 13
- Multiple Choice Questions 14
- True/False Questions 15
- Matching Questions 15

Overcoming Test Anxiety 16

Unit One: The Nature and History of Psychology 19
- Learning Objectives 19
- Definition and Goals of Psychology 19
  - Structuralism and Wundt 20
  - Functionalism and James 20
  - Gestalt Psychology 21
  - Pavlov and Classical Conditioning 21
  - Watson, Skinner, and Behaviorism 21
  - Freud and the Psychodynamic Perspective 21
  - Humanistic Psychology 22
  - Biological Perspective 22
  - Evolutionary Psychology 22
  - Cognitive Perspective 22
  - Sociocultural Perspective 23
- Research Methods 23
  - Case Study 23
  - Naturalistic Observation 24
  - Correlational Research 24
  - Survey Research 24
  - Experiment 25

- Tests 25
  - Statistical Methods 26
  - Psychological Specialties 27
- Unit One Practice Quiz 29
- Unit Two: Biological Influences on Behavior 31
  - Learning Objectives 31
  - Genes, Evolution, and Environment 31
  - Environmental Influences 33
  - Nervous System 34
- Unit Two Practice Quiz 42
- Unit Three: Sensation and Perception 44
  - Learning Objectives 44
  - Psychophysics and Thresholds 44
  - Sensory Adaptation 44
  - Vision 45
  - Hearing 45
  - Taste 46
  - Smell 46
  - Skin Senses 47
  - Basic Perceptual Phenomena 47
  - Influences on Perception 49
  - Subliminal Perception 49
  - Extrasensory Perception 49
- Unit Three Practice Quiz 50
- Unit Four: Consciousness 52
  - Learning Objectives 52
  - Biological Rhythms 52
  - Sleep 52
  - Hypnosis 54
  - Psychoactive Drugs 54
- Unit Four Practice Quiz 56
- Unit Five: Learning and Memory 58
  - Learning Objectives 58

- Learning 58
- Memory 61
- Memory as a Reconstructive Process 61
- Unit Five Practice Quiz 65
- Unit Six: Motivation and Emotion 67
  - Learning Objectives 67
  - Specific Motives 67
- Unit Six Practice Quiz 73
- Unit Seven: Thinking and Intelligence 75
  - Learning Objectives 75
- Unit Seven Practice Quiz 75
- Unit Eight: Human Development 75
  - Learning Objectives 75
- Unit Eight Practice Quiz 75
- Unit Nine: Personality 75
  - Learning Objectives 75
  - Theories of Personality 75
- Unit Nine Practice Quiz 75
- Unit Ten: Psychological Disorders and Therapies 75
  - Learning Objectives 75
- Unit Ten Practice Quiz 75
- Unit Eleven: Social Psychology 75
  - Learning Objectives 75
  - Behavior in Social and Cultural Context 75
- Unit Eleven Practice Quiz 75
- Practice Test 75
- Practice Exam Answer Key 75

Preparing for Your Exam

Chances are if you are reading this, you are a student looking to perform well on an upcoming test. Congratulations, you have taken the first step in achieving that goal. Yes, you have purchased this text, but more importantly this means you have determined to seek success and do what it takes to achieve this success. This means you are already in the right mindset to begin…so why don't we do just that and get started?

Taking a test and performing well is much like a sport. Consider the test to be the "big game" that students face over and over. Every athlete knows the importance of preparing for the game through practice, drills, and training. Just preparing is not enough, the athlete also knows the rules for his or her chosen sport and has developed the ability to remain calm under pressure. Each of these three skills comes together to allow the athlete to perform to the best of their ability and hopefully win the "big game". As a student, you have no doubt heard more than once those tests are designed to demonstrate your knowledge of the subject matter, and while that is true, this is not the entire picture. We have all encountered that student who studies less than everyone yet manages to pass or even get an "A" on the tests they take. Chances are this student not only knows the subject matter, but they know how to play the game. This text is designed to help you understand those "rules" and develop skills that will make you a master test taker. This guide will in no way substitute for knowledge of subject matter, but will certainly assist you in making sure that your test accurately demonstrates that knowledge and that the "rules of the game" operate in your favor. As we move forward, we are going to analyze some study skills that will help you acquire the subject matter knowledge necessary for your test, learn a few test-taking skills that will help you "play the game" even better, and examine how to work well under pressure (relive some of the test anxiety).

Study Skills

Ask almost anyone and they will tell you that the key to success on a test is to know the subject materials for which you are being tested. As we already mentioned, this is only part of the puzzle, but it is an important part. Thus, it is where we will begin our journey together – how to best acquire this subject matter expertise. Our goal here is to help you make the most of the time you invest for studying so that you gain the most knowledge possible in the time you commit to studying.

One of the most important things you can do, as a student, is to determine your learning style. This knowledge will serve you not only for this test, but for every class you ever take. There are a myriad of online quizzes that will help you identify your learning style, but for the sake of brevity we are going to discuss the five basic learning styles here. Chances are you already know how you learn best, even if you have never formally addressed this topic. The five learning styles are described below.

1. Visual learning – has a preference for learning through pictures, graphs, and spatial understanding.
2. Auditory – sometimes called musical – learns best through sound and lectures.
3. Verbal – sometimes called linguistic – process information through words both verbal and written.
4. Kinesthetic – this learner processes by feeling, sensing, and doing
5. Logical – sometimes called mathematical – uses logic and reasoning

If you are a **visual** learner you will want to spend time making graphs, charts, timelines, maps, and pictures that will help you understand the materials. You are going to remember far more about a picture, than information you simply read. If you are an **auditory** learner, then you are one in a small percentage of students who actually do learn through the lecture model that most of western education is built upon. The auditory learner will do best by reading texts books aloud so that they are not simply reading, but hearing the text. Much like the auditory learner, the **verbal** learner should also read test materials aloud. In this case, it is not hearing the content, but in verbalizing it. In addition to spoken word, the verbal learner also learns well by writing information. This makes the practice of note-taking especially beneficial to this learner. The **kinesthetic** learner is often the most challenging for teachers and professors to address. It is the kinesthetic learner who learns best by actually "doing". If you are this type of learner then you need to feel, hold, and manipulate objects in order to best understand the content. This type of learner will learn better while moving around and seldom studies well at a typical desk. Finally, the **logical** learner, needs to understand the "why" behind ideas and concepts. The logical learner needs to see connections and reasons behind the information. Memorization of facts does not typically serve the logical learner as well as a thorough understanding of how the concepts relate to one another. It is important to note here that while one primary sense is usually tied to your learning style, you should incorporate as many senses as possible into your learning routine. So for the visual learner, it is imperative that they see the information in displayed form, but they will also enhance their memory be utilizing their auditory, verbal, and kinesthetic skills. Remember the more senses you can involve in the learning process the better. Don't be afraid to draw, read aloud, sing, or create objects that can be moved in order to see the logic and connections behind the facts.

In addition to the five different learning styles, there are two additional styles that some authors have added. These two are the solitary and social learner. These two types of learners can be found in conjunction with any of the above five learning styles. For example, one could be a solitary visual learner. As the name implies, the solitary learner prefers to learn alone while the social learner prefers learning in the group setting. While the solitary learner is likely to be found alone in the library, the social learner gravitates toward study groups and enjoys group projects that the solitary learner often dreads.

There has been much debate over the years regarding the best time of day to study. The short answer is, there is no one correct answer. The best time of day for study is completely student dependent. If an individual is more alert in the morning then they should study in the morning. If the student is better in the evening, then study in the evening. Most fathers are fond of reminding their children that "you can't hoot with the owls and soar with the eagles."

Of course, the preference is typically that you soar with the morning eagles and avoid the night owls as much as possible. However, the main idea serves as a great reminder for students – if you are a morning person make sure to get enough rest to rise early and make use of that time. If you are indeed a night owl, then sleep in and be sure you devote the evening time to study, not just socializing with friends.

With the preliminaries out of the way, let us dive into some more hands on considerations that will help you make the most of your study time.

1. Prepare your space –
   a. Do not study in your bed. Our bodies are conditioned to see the bed as a place of rest and relaxation. By attempting to study in bed, we are constantly fighting the ingrained habit of our bodies. In addition, it can be difficult to fight the constant temptation to take a "quick cat nap" that turns into an hour or two of lost time.
   b. If you do not study in bed, where should you study? Really just about anywhere else that works for you and fits your learning style. Consider a dedicated space that you use only for study. The more you use the space the more your brain will begin to equate the space with productive study.
   c. For most students, a desk really is the best option as it not only sets the tone for study and work but also promotes good posture. Many kinesthetic learners benefit from a standing desk or a chair that allows for movement.
   d. Consider the lighting. Select a space that has good natural light and allows for good artificial light to be added if studying at night. In seeking natural light be cautious of windows. While they do provide great natural light, they can also be a source of distraction. If possible consider this in the placement of your desk. Desks placed to the side of a window allow for good light, but the temptation to gaze into the outdoors is limited by not being situated directly in front of you.
   e. Gather all your materials. Make sure you study space is adequately stocked with all the necessary materials: books, pens and pencils, paper, computer, printer, etc.
   f. Select appropriate music. For most learning styles, music that is instrumental is best for learning. This prevents one from using part of the brain to sing along instead of being focused on the topic at hand. For the auditory or musical learner, music can be especially powerful as subject material can be tied to the music for better understanding and recall.

2. Create a schedule for study. Determine what topics will be covered by your test and how many days you have to study for the exam. Plan out what topics you will study each day in order to be prepared for the test. Do not plan on studying any new material the night before the exam, as cramming is never a good option. Be sure to devote more time to topics that are unfamiliar or difficult.

3. Use a timer. Set your timer for 20 or 25 minutes. Studies show that the optimal time to study is in 20 to 25 minute segments with a 5 to 10 minute break between each. Your brain is actually best at remembering the first and last thing that you study. Therefore these short segments give you more first and last items. These short segments are short enough to maintain attention (even for those with ADD or ADHD) and long enough to study a substantial amount of information. During your break get up and move around. Be sure your whole body is involved. The physical activity keeps your blood flowing and gives your brain a chance to take a break, without shutting down completely.

4. Study in "chunks". As we mentioned earlier your brain is great at remembering the first and last items on which you focus attention. Use this fact to your advantage by breaking information into lists or chunks of 3 to 5 items. This allows for more first and lasts in the set of information and uses your brains built in systems to your advantage.

5. Concentrate. It seems like the simplest advice, but the importance of concentration cannot be overstated. Concentration is the self-discipline of studying. Studying is not a passive skill (as much as all students wish it was). Studying is an active sport. You must engage your brain. If you struggle with concentration or suffer from ADD / ADHD consider removing anything that might distract you. For this author this meant going to the top floor of the library where the "quite rule" was strictly enforced, finding an enclosed study area where there were no visual distractions, and putting earplugs in so that not even the turning of pages could distract me. It soon became apparent that an hour spent in this environment was far more productive than 2 or 3 hours trying to study in a dorm room or even a more social area of the library. Do not be afraid to do what it takes to make concentration easier, it is a difficult discipline to build.

6. DO NOT use a highlighter when studying. A highlighter may be beneficial in marking items to be studied at a later time, but that is precisely what makes it such a poor tool for studying. The best use for a highlighter is in a fast paced lecture when something needs to be noted for later study. However, when studying as an individual the highlighter often serves as a mark of procrastination. Instead of highlighting the text to come back to later, take the time to devote it to memory. If the information is too in-depth or is a bit off topic, make a note on a separate piece of paper to come back and study further. The simple act of writing it down instead of highlighting begins the learning process. Make every attempt to understand and process information before moving along to another topic and instead of highlighting for later study.

7. Create connections. The more you can connect a new concept to something you already know the better your learning and recall will be. For visual learners, these connections should be drawn in pictures, flow charts or graphs. For the kinesthetic

learner, as much as possible, the connections should be acted out or put into motions.

8. Use all of your senses. As much as possible try to engage all of your senses when studying. It is understood that your sight is always part of studying. Include your speech (which we know is not a true sense) and hearing in your study. Instead of just reading material silently "in your head", read it out loud. This engages three aspects of your brain: sight, hearing, and speech which makes it more likely you will remember the content. If there is a way you can integrate the whole body into the concept then do so.

9. Study items from broad concepts to minor details. As you begin to study, tackle the major points first. If you understand how whole chapters relate to one another then adding the smaller details will be easier.

10. Always focus on the bold print or italicized words in a text, as these are strong indicators of important material.

11. When you study consider using the same pen / pencil for all study related to this test and then take this pencil with you to the testing center. As you study play a mental trick on yourself by storing all the answers you write into your pencil. With that pencil with you at the exam, you have already written all the answers you are going to need. Sure it is a mental trick, but you have actually studied hard and written all the answers you are going to need. The mental trick simply serves as a psychological reminder to this fact.

12. Use flash cards. Sometimes there is information that simply must be devoted to memory (formulas, historical events, lists, vocabulary). For this type of information use flash cards. Three by five index cards work well. Put the definition or name of the formula on the front of the card and the answer on the back. Quiz yourself using the cards and reviewing the cards you missed in each set before attempting to work through the entire deck again. Flash cards work great for reviewing materials when you only have a few moments (perhaps between classes, or waiting in line).

13. Use mnemonic techniques to memorize materials. There are several mnemonic techniques that work well depending on the situation.
    a. For key words or lists consider using an ACRONYM to remember the list. An acronym is an invented combination of letters. If you have ever had the pleasure of playing a musical instrument you probably remember your grade school music teacher saying Every Good Boy Does Fine in an effort to help you remember the order of the notes on the clef scale.
    b. Another option for lists or key words is the ACROSTIC - You probably remember Please Excuse My Dear Aunt Sally from grade school when your teacher used it to help you remember the order of operations: Parenthesis, Exponents, Multiply, Divide, Addition, Subtraction.

c. Location method – this method involves using a specific location to tie concepts together. For this example let us assume we are trying to memorize the following short list of landforms: hill, mountain, and plateau. We might picture our living room and imagine that as we walk in the door we are met immediately by a hill we must crawl over, followed by a television displaying a picture of the mountain. Lastly sitting there on the sofa is a plateau (you may even picture your uncle who has the flat buzz cut to help you remember the flat plateau). The more vivid you make the pictures the better and easier to remember them they will be.

d. Rhyming Method – This is a two-step method in which you create words that rhyme with numbers and then build an association with those words. This method works best for ordered lists. For example if you were going to remember the following items for a grocery list: milk, bread, eggs, cheese, and chicken. To remember the first item on the list we would find a word that rhymes with "one". For our case, we will choose "run". You are going to picture yourself running and carrying a gallon of milk. Much like the Location method, the trick to making this particular mnemonic device work is to make the picture and relationship between the two words as vivid as possible. So instead of just picturing yourself running with a gallon of milk in hand, you will picture yourself running while pouring the milk over your head. You could even get some of your other senses involved by imagining the smell of the milk to be putrid due to the hot weather in which you are running. By involving more senses and making the picture more vivid you are far less likely to forget the milk when you arrive at the store. This process would be repeated using the next number in the sequence and so on for each item that needs to be memorized.

14. Study groups – If you are a social learner then you will certainly benefit from the advantages that study groups offer. However, be prepared when you arrive and do not expect the study group to replace individual effort needed to learn new material. Study groups typically work best, for both social and solitary learners as a place to test knowledge. By quizzing one another, students can become more confident about material they know and find out what concepts may need a bit more attention. In addition, study groups can often help the student who is stumped on a particular concept. Do not be afraid to ask for study group members to explain something or help you understand it more clearly. Often hearing something described in different words is just the key our brain needs to unlock the information fully.

Scheduling Your Test

It may seem like a simplistic reminder, but if you are a morning person you will want to schedule your exam for the morning hours. Be sure to give yourself adequate time to get up, get ready and face any traffic on your way to the testing center. If you are better in the evenings, schedule the time that is near the end of the day but NOT the last session. Think back to elementary school and the fear of being the last person to turn in their test while others waited for you. You do not want the added stress of those around you leaving while you needlessly fear being the only person left.

Last Minute Preparation for Testing

You have studied as much as possible and tomorrow is the big day. What should you do tonight to make sure you are prepared for the big test? Let us begin with the one thing you should NOT do. Do not get caught up in cramming or even reviewing one last time. It is actually too late for that to do you much good. Tonight you should relax and focus on just a few items.

1. Get to bed early (or at least not excessively late) so you will be fresh for your test.

2. Use this time for positive self-talk. Remind yourself how much you have studied for this exam and how prepared you are to show just how well you know the information.

3. The night before set out the items you will need for testing. Lay out clothing you plan to wear (go for comfort over style here). Make sure you include a jacket / hoodie as most testing centers tend to stay cold to help you stay awake. In addition, be sure your photo ID, pencils, calculator, and other requirements for the test are ready to be grabbed as you walk out the door.

4. Eat breakfast. Sure this is motherly advice, but it is good advice. Your brain needs fuel to function. Make sure you feed it. Avoid sugary foods that will leave you in a slump later and impact concentration levels. High protein foods are best as they help provide long-term energy.

5. Visit the restroom 15 – 20 minutes before the test and refrain from drinking fluids within an hour of your test.

6. Arrive 10-15 minutes early for the test so you do not have the stress of being late.

7. During the last few minutes, it is okay to review a formula or fact sheet of information you have dedicated to memory. One of the first things you will do when you sit for the exam, is to "dump" this information onto your scrap paper. Note that this is not the time to "cram" this information into your brain. It should already be memorized; you are just reviewing one last time.

8. Before you are seated for the exam take a few deep breaths and relax. If you are subject to test anxiety we will cover more on how to relax a bit later.

Test-Taking Tips

When we began this text we explained that taking a test was much like a sport and that understanding the rules of the game (test-taking skills) were just as important as ability to play (subject matter knowledge). In the next several pages we are going to explore ways you can put the rules of the game to work for you. By understanding and applying these test-taking strategies you improve your odds for success.

The number one tip for taking a test is to **remain confident**. It is amazing how confidence can change the outcome of situations. If you have studied adequately your hard work will pay off when it comes to taking the test. Just relax and trust yourself. If you suffer from test anxiety this tip is even more important. (See also the tips for test anxiety a few pages later.)

Once you begin the test and the timer begins, **take the first few moments to write down any formulas, dates, facts that you have dedicated to memory**, but are not included on a "fact sheet" for the exam. Doing this "brain dump" allows your brain to figuratively free up space that was being used to hold this information. It also ensures you do not forget the information later down the road when you need it.

Before you begin, take a look at the entire test and determine how you will **budget your time**. Often tests are computerized so this does not mean to click through every question, but simply learning how many questions there are so that you can stay on target to finish in the time allotted.

It often goes without saying, but it should not, that you need to **read the instructions**. You have probably had that teacher that gave you the following directions test that asked you to read the whole test before marking any answers and the result likely resulted in hilarity as your classmates did silly things because they didn't read the directions. (You would never fall for that trick yourself). While this is not elementary school and a standardized test is not going to set out to confuse you with directions, they are no less important. The difference between understanding mark the "best" answer and "only" answer can save you a great deal of confusion, and the difference between writing an essay about all of the topics or choosing a topic can mean the difference in passing and failing. So as elementary and boring as it is, take time to read the directions.

After reading the directions, you will want to **begin with the easiest questions** first. Most tests today are written in increased order of difficulty so this is typically the way you approach the test anyway. Answering easy questions will serve to boost your self-confidence and prepare you for the harder questions to come. However, if you encounter a problem that "stumps" you do not be afraid to leave it unanswered and return to it at a later time. Be sure you either mark the question on the test or make note on your scrap paper so you do not submit the test with an unanswered question. A question may often have clues to other questions within it.

As you answer questions **rely on your first impressions** and do not overthink the answers. Unless you are 100% sure that you have the wrong answer and are 100% that the answer you are changing to is the correct answer do not deviate from your initial "gut reaction". Teachers would be quite wealthy if rewarded every time a student admitted to changing from a correct to incorrect answer. Do not be that student. Go with your first instincts unless you are absolutely sure you were wrong.

If you finish early, **use the time to review** your answers. Check to be sure you answered all of the questions. Proofread any essays for spelling and grammatical errors. If the test covered mathematics, check your calculations and use the calculator if it is acceptable to do so.

Multiple Choice Questions

Depending on the type of test you are likely to encounter different types of questions. Each of these question types has specific strategies that will help you in taking tests. The most common type of test question for standardized tests is the **multiple-choice** test. Consider these strategies for these types of questions:

1. Before reading the answers to a multiple-choice question try to formulate the answer on your own. This adds confidence to your answer and ensures your brain is engaged in the answering process.

2. While you should formulate your own answer before reading the choices, be sure you read all of the answers before selecting your answer.

3. Statements that begin with concrete exceptions: never, none, always, except, most, least, are likely not the answer.

4. Eliminate unlikely answers. If you can reduce the possible answers to 2 you increase your odds of selecting the right answer or even guessing correctly.

5. If you must guess, consider these guidelines:
   a. If there are two answers that are opposites from one another then the answer is likely one of those two answers.
   b. If there are two answers that are very similar, it is likely that the answer is neither of the two.
   c. Typically the longer and more descriptive answer is the correct answer
   d. If your answers are numbers then it is likely that the answer lies in the middle of the range of answers, not at the extremes. For example, if you answers are:
      a) 100   b) 10   c) 9   d) 0.02

   You would eliminate the 100 and .02 and then determine if the answer is either 9 or 10. Again this is not always correct but helps in a situation where you may be forced to guess.

6. Be sure you answer every question. Most tests do not penalize you for guessing so it is best to answer every question even if guessing. Research your specific test for rules about penalties for wrong answers so you know how to approach guessing.

7. Watch out for questions that ask for opposites such as "which of the following is NOT" or "Which statement is false." These questions require reverse thinking.

True/False Questions

While it is not common for standardized tests to have questions other than multiple choice, sometimes you may encounter True/False questions. For **True/False** questions consider the following tips.

1. Look at specific details. Specific details tend to make the statement true. For example, The Empire State Building is 1,250 feet tall. The detail of 1250 feet is a very specific detail and chances are this test question is TRUE.

2. When forced to guess, choose TRUE. More questions tend to be true than false, as most instructors and test writers find it more difficult to write statements that are false.

3. Look for extreme words such as: all, always, only, nobody, everybody, absolutely, etc. These words tend be used in statements that are FALSE.

4. Look for qualifying words such as: seldom, often, many, seldom, much, sometimes, etc. These words tend to make the statement TRUE.

5. Look for reasons. If the statement includes a reason it tends to be FALSE. Words like since, because, when, and if add justification or reasoning to the statement and tend to make it FALSE. Also check the justification to make sure it is complete. An incomplete justification makes the statement FALSE.

6. Look for negative words such as: not, none, or no. Also check for negative prefixes such as *un-,im-, miss-*. These negatives can confuse the statement and should be treated with caution.

Matching Questions

Sometimes you will encounter matching questions. These will often appear in a format very similar to multiple choice questions, but should be treated a bit differently. Here are a few tips to help you navigate these types of questions.

1. Read the directions carefully. Sometimes matching answers may be used only once, in other questions the answers may be used more than once. This certainly makes guessing much more difficult if there are answers that can be used more than once.

2. Look at both "sides" or sets of answers / questions. Get an idea of what the relationships might be between the two groups.

3. Use one list to find matches on the second list. This will keep confusion to a minimum.

4. Check the entire second "side" before selecting answers. There may be a more correct answer that follows.

5. Cross off matches on the second "side" in order to make finding subsequent matches easier.

6. Do not make a guess until you have worked through the entire first "side" one time completely.

Overcoming Test Anxiety

One of the most debilitating problems a student can face is test anxiety. Test anxiety can manifest itself through tense muscles, fast heart and breathing rate, cramps, and even nausea. The student who suffers from test anxiety often knows the material as well as, or better than his or her classmates, but this never shows up on tests because the anxiety takes over. It is important for those who suffer from test anxiety to remain calm and confident. There are also other ways to help the brain and body cope with this type of anxiety.

1. **Breathe**. Breathing is not only essential to our existence, but serves as a way of relaxing the mind and body. Purposefully taking a few deep breaths can do a great deal to bring calm to the body. When you feel anxiety about to take over, begin to breathe deeply and calmly. Three to five deep breaths normally do the trick and can be repeated as often as necessary.

2. **Relax**. There will be times during the test that you begin to feel anxious. Recognize this feeling. Does it begin with tightening of the shoulders and neck or does it start in your stomach and slowly take over your body? Become aware of the feelings and the how they start. When you feel that trigger or beginning feeling consciously focus on relaxation. There are many great books and websites dedicated to relaxation techniques. Explore and find one that works best for you.

3. **Take practice tests.** Before you sit for the actual exam, take as many practice exams as you can. Make the surroundings as much like the test center as you can. Give yourself the same time limits, and breaks you will be taking during the exam. The more you can make the practice seem like a test, the more the test will seem like practice. This brings us to the next point.

4. **Think of the test as practice.** This author, once had a student who scored a 32 on a quiz that covered multiplication facts all of which the student had recited the day before. It was apparent the student had become more and more anxious during the exam. As the class was assigned a new worksheet, this student was given the same quiz with one slight change made. At the top of the page, the word "Quiz" was replaced by "Practice". Guess what he made on the "Practice" sheet? You guessed it; he made a 100. Sure it is going to be hard to convince yourself that the test you are going to take at a testing center is really a "Practice" sheet, but there is no reason that you cannot retake the test. Most CLEP and standardized tests allow you to reset for the exam in 6 months (some less). Sure that is a while to wait and you do not want to stress over this test again, but remind yourself this is not the only shot you have at this. Take some of the pressure off of yourself.

5. **Do not panic.** Chances are that if you suffer from test anxiety you are already well acquainted with panic. Simply do not give into it. Force yourself to relax while reminding yourself of your confidence through positive self-talk.

6. **Stay Positive.** Remind yourself of how much you are prepared for this and that a poor exam score only results from many missed questions not one or two.

7. **Stay Realistic.** As we just mentioned one wrong answer does not mean you will fail the exam. Remind yourself that you simply need to pass. No one needs to know your score; you just need to do well enough to pass the exam. As you continue with positive self-talk do not let one or two questions send you into a spiral of self-doubt and more anxiety. Stay realistic about outcomes and your performance.

8. **Take care of yourself.** This is the most often overlooked advice when it comes to test anxiety. Your body is much more likely to respond appropriately if you are treating it appropriately by eating healthy foods and exercising regularly. In addition, regular exercise is shown to reduce stress and is a great way to build up tolerance and coping skills for test anxiety.

As you prepare for your upcoming exam, realized there are no shortcuts to doing well on a test. There is no replacement for knowledge of this subject matter, but hopefully the study skills mentioned here will help you make the most of your time spent studying. As you take the test remember the test- taking skills, as these will help you demonstrate your true mastery of the subject matter. Before you set for the exam and anxiety takes over be sure to put into practice some of the tactics we have mentioned for overcoming anxiety. If you already know what techniques work well for you those techniques will be at your disposal during the test.

Remember that just as the athlete must not only has mastery of the sport but must understand the rules and remain calm under pressure so must you the test-taker. It is important that you master all three skills as each plays a part in your success. You may not be scoring goals, sinking baskets, or serving aces, but you are going to win this game called test-taking. Just remember to have confidence in yourself.

Unit One: The Nature and History of Psychology

Learning Objectives
After completing Unit One, you should be able to:

1. Describe and explain the definition and goal of psychology
2. Discuss the history of psychology
3. Discuss the different perspectives on behavior
4. Discuss the scientific principles of psychology
5. Discuss the different methods of research
6. Discuss the different specialties in psychology

Definition and Goals of Psychology

Psychology is the scientific study of behavior and the mind. The term 'behavior' refers to actions and responses that we can directly observe, whereas the term 'mind' refers to internal states and processes, such as thoughts and feelings that cannot be seen directly and that must be inferred from observable, measurable responses. Psychology began as an attempt to answer philosophical questions about human nature, using methods borrowed from physics, physiology, and other sciences. Psychology's systematic approach yields more accurate knowledge about behavior than do everyday casual observations and conventional folk wisdom, which have generated many misconceptions and myths about human nature.

As a science, psychology has four central goals: description, explanation, control, and application.

- **Description** is the most basic goal. Psychologists seek to describe how people behave, think, and feel.
- **Explanation** typically takes the form of hypotheses and theories which specify the causes of behavior, as psychologists strive to explain and to understand why people act as they do.
- **Control** is where psychologists design experiments or other types of research to test the accuracy of their proposed explanations.
- **Application** is where psychologists apply psychological knowledge in ways that enhance human welfare.

Science involves both basic research, which reflects the quest for knowledge for its own sake, and applied research, which focuses on solving practical problems. For psychologists, most research examines how and why people behave, think, and feel the way they do.

History of Psychology

Humans have long sought to understand themselves, and for ages, the mind-body problem has occupied the center of this quest. Many early philosophers held a position of mind-body dualism, the belief that the mind is a spiritual entity not subject to physical laws that govern the body. Dualism implies that no amount of research on the physical body, including the brain, could ever hope to unravel the mysteries of the nonphysical mind.

Another view is that of monism, which holds that the mind and body are one and that the mind is not a separate spiritual entity. To monists, mental events correspond to physical events in the brain. Monism helped set the stage for psychology because it implied that the mind could be studied by measuring physical processes within the brain.

Discoveries in physiology (an area of biology that examines bodily functioning) and medicine helped pave the way for psychology's emergence. Several major perspectives have shaped psychology's scientific growth.

Structuralism and Wundt

The infant science of psychology emerged in 1879, when Wilhelm Wundt established the first experimental psychology laboratory at the University of Leipzig in Germany. He believed that the mind could be studied by breaking it down into basic components, as a chemist might break down a complex chemical compound. This approach came to be known as structuralism, which is the analysis of the mind in terms of its basic elements. In their experiments, structuralists used the method of introspection (looking within) to study sensations and reporting on one's own conscious thoughts and feelings, which they considered the basic elements of consciousness. Structuralism left an important mark by establishing a scientific tradition for studying cognitive processes.

Functionalism and James

In the United States, structuralism eventually gave way to functionalism, which held that psychology should study the functions of consciousness rather than its elements. Functionalism was influenced by Darwin's evolutionary theory, which stressed the importance of adaptation in helping organisms survive and reproduce in their environment. William James, a leader in the functionalist movement, taught courses in physiology and psychology at Harvard University.

James helped widen the scope of psychology to include the study of various biological and mental processes and overt behavior. Although functionalism no longer exists as a school of thought within psychology, its tradition endures in two modern-day fields: cognitive psychology, which studies mental processes, and evolutionary psychology, which emphasizes the adaptiveness of behavior.

Gestalt Psychology

By the 1920s, German scientists had formed a school of thought known as Gestalt psychology, which examined how the mind organizes elements of experience into a unified or whole perception. They argued that perceptions are organized so that the whole is greater than the sum of its parts. Gestalt psychology stimulated interest in topics such as perception and problem solving.

Pavlov and Classical Conditioning

In the early 1900s, experiments by Russian physiologist Ivan Pavlov revealed how learning occurs when events are associated with one another. Pavlov found that dogs automatically learned to salivate to the sound of a new stimulus, such as a tone or bell, if that stimulus was repeatedly paired with a known stimulus, such as food. This particular type of psychology examines how organisms learn through the consequences of their actions. Thus, learning is the key to understanding how experience molds behavior.

Watson, Skinner, and Behaviorism

The behavioral perspective emphasizes how the external environment and learning shape behavior. Watson and Skinner believed that psychology should study only observable stimuli and responses, not unobservable mental processes. Behaviorism is a school of thought which emphasizes environmental control of behavior through learning. Behaviorists sought to discover laws that govern learning, and they believed that the same basic principles of learning applied to all organisms.

Skinner was a leading 20th century behaviorist who believed that the real causes of behavior reside in the outer world: "A person does not act upon the world, the world acts upon him". Skinner believed that through social engineering, society could harness the power of the environment to change behavior in beneficial ways. His approach, known as radical behaviorism, was esteemed for its scientific contributions and for focusing attention on how environmental forces could be used to enhance human welfare.

Freud and the Psychodynamic Perspective

The psychodynamic perspective searches for the causes of behavior within the inner workings of our personality (our unique pattern of traits, emotions, and motives), emphasizing the role of unconscious processes. Sigmund Freud developed the first and most influential psychodynamic theory. Freud was convinced that an unconscious part of the mind profoundly influences behavior, and he developed a theory and form of psychotherapy called psychoanalysis - the analysis of internal and primary unconscious psychological forces.

Freud also proposed that humans have powerful inborn sexual and aggressive drives and that, because these desires are punished in childhood, we learn to fear them and become anxious when we are aware of their presence. This leads us to develop defense mechanisms, which are psychological techniques that help us cope with anxiety and the pain of traumatic experiences.

Repression, a primary defense mechanism, protects us by keeping unacceptable impulses, feelings, and memories in the unconscious depths of the mind. All behavior, whether normal or abnormal, reflects a largely unconscious and inevitable conflict between the defenses and internal impulses.

Humanistic Psychology

The humanistic perspective emphasizes free will, personal growth, and the attempt to find meaning in one's existence. The humanistic perspective emphasizes personal freedom and choice, personal growth, and self-actualization. Abraham Maslow was a humanistic theorist who proposed that each of us has an inborn force toward self-actualization, the reaching of one's individual potential. When people develop in a supportive environment, their positive inner nature emerges.

Biological Perspective

The biological perspective examines how brain processes and other bodily functions regulate behavior and psychological characteristics. Behavioral neuroscientists study brain activity and hormonal influences; behavior geneticists examine the role of heredity; and evolutionary psychologists seek to explain how evolution has biologically predisposed modern humans toward certain ways of behaving.

Evolutionary Psychology

Evolutionary psychology seeks to explain how evolution shaped modern behavior. Evolutionary psychologists stress that human mental abilities and behavioral tendencies evolved along with a changing body. According to one theory, as our humanlike ancestors developed new physical abilities, they began to use tools and weapons and live in social groups.

In his theory of evolution, Darwin noted that within a species some members possess specific traits to a greater extent than do other members. Through a process he called natural selection, if an inherited trait gives certain members an advantage over others, these members will be more likely to survive and pass these characteristics on to their offspring. In this way, species evolve as the presence of adaptive traits increases within the population over generations. Thus, through natural selection, adaptations to new environmental demands contributed to the development of the brain, just as the brain growth contributed to the further development of human behavior.

Cognitive Perspective

The cognitive perspective, embodied by the subfield of cognitive psychology, views humans as information processors who think, judge, and solve problems. Cognitive neuroscience examines brain processes that occur as people perform mental tasks. This perspective views the human as a thinker, studying a person's thoughts, anticipations, planning, perceptions, attention, and memory processes.

Sociocultural Perspective

The sociocultural perspective examines how the social environment and cultural learning influence our behavior and thoughts. Cultural psychologists study how culture is transmitted to members of society and examine similarities and differences among people from various cultures. This perspective studies the human as a social being embedded in a culture, and assesses social forces, including norms, social interactions, and group processes in one's culture and social environment.

Research Methods

Because psychology is a science, information about human behavior is collected in systematic, objective, and replicable ways - primarily through experimental and correlation studies. Whenever possible, scientists prefer to test their understanding of "what causes what" more directly. If we truly understand the causes of a given behavior, then we should be able to predict the conditions under which that behavior will occur in the future. Furthermore, if we can control those conditions, then we should be able to produce that behavior. Psychologists conduct research to gather evidence about behavior and its causes. The research method chosen depends on the problem being studied, the investigator's objectives, and ethical principles.

Case Study

A case study is an in-depth analysis of an individual, a group, or event. By studying a single case in detail, researchers typically hope to discover principles that hold true for people or situations in general. Data may be gathered through observation, interviews, psychological tests, physiological recordings, or task performance. Case studies have several advantages and disadvantages:

Advantages:
- When a rare phenomenon occurs, this method enables scientists to study it closely.
- A case study may challenge the validity of a theory or scientific belief.
- A case study can be a source of new ideas that may be examined using other research methods.

Disadvantages:
- The major limitation of a case study is that it is a poor method for determining cause-effect relationships because, in most studies, explanations of behaviors occur after the fact and there is little opportunity to rule out alternative explanations.
- A second problem concerns the generalizability of the findings, meaning, will the principles uncovered in a case study hold true for other people or in other situations.
- A third problem is the possible lack of objectivity in the way data are gathered and interpreted, because case studies are often based on the researcher's subjective impressions.

Naturalistic Observation

The researcher observes behavior as it occurs in a natural setting, and attempts to avoid influencing that behavior. Naturalistic observation is used to study human behavior. Naturalistic observation can yield rich descriptions of behavior in real-life settings and permits examination of relations between variables.

Like case studies, naturalistic observation does not permit clear causal conclusions. In the real world, many variables simultaneously influence behavior, and they cannot be disentangled with this type of research technique. There is also the possibility of bias in how researchers interpret what they observe. Finally, the presence of an observer may disrupt a person's or animal's behavior.

Correlational Research

This type of research involves assessing the relationship between two variables. Because neither variable is manipulated, there is no way to determine if changes in one variable cause changes in the other. Only how changes in one are related to changes in the other can be determined. A positive relationship means that high scores in one variable tend to be paired with high scores in the other variable. A negative relationship means that high scores in one variable tend to be paired with low scores in the other variable. In addition to the direction of the relationship, a correlation coefficient will describe the strength of the relationship.

The benefits of conducting correlational research include: establishing if relations found in the laboratory generalize to the outside world, and discovering associations that are subsequently studied under controlled laboratory conditions. Moreover, for practical or ethical reasons, some questions cannot be studied with experiments but can be examined in a correlational study, and correlation data allows us to make predictions.

Survey Research

Information about a topic is obtained by administering questionnaires to or conducting interviews with many people. In survey research, a population consists of all the individuals who are the target of the study. Because it is often impractical to study an entire population, a survey is administered to a sample group, which is a subset of individuals drawn from a larger population. To draw valid conclusions about a population from a survey, the sample must be representative. A representative sample is one that reflects the important characteristics of a population.

When a representative sample is surveyed, the researcher can be confident that the findings closely portray those of the population as a whole. This is the strongest advantage of survey research. In scientific research, surveys are an efficient method for collecting a large amount of information about people's opinions, experiences, and lifestyles, and they can reveal changes in people's beliefs and habits over many years.

Some of the drawbacks to survey research are that: survey data cannot be used to draw conclusions about cause and effect; surveys rely on participants self-reports, which can be distorted by bias; and under-representative samples can lead to faulty generalizations about how an entire population would respond.

Experiment

In experiments, researchers assess cause and effect relationships between at least two variables. The cause is represented by the independent variable and will always involve treating subjects in at least two different ways. Subjects in the experimental group are exposed to whatever the presumed "cause" is; those in the control group are not exposed to the "cause." The "effect" is represented by the dependent variable and will typically involve measuring how subjects behave. Because subjects are assigned randomly to each experimental condition, and because there is only one difference in how the experiment and control groups are treated, any difference in the behavior of those two groups must be due to that treatment (i.e., the independent variable). An experiment has three essential characteristics:

- The researcher manipulates one or more variables. The independent variable refers to the factor that is manipulated or controlled by the experimenter.
- The researcher measures whether this manipulation influences other variables. The dependent variable is the factor that is measured by the experimenter and may be influenced by the independent variable.
- The researcher attempts to control extraneous factors that might influence the outcome of the experiment.

The independent variable is viewed as the cause and the dependent variable as the effect. It is possible that subjects in an experimental group could behave differently than they normally would, because they know they are being exposed to special treatment. This is called the placebo effect. In order to determine the extent to which this might be happening, the control group subjects are sometimes told that they too are receiving a special treatment or drug, even when they are not. This fake special treatment or drug is called a placebo. If subjects don't know whether or not they are receiving the placebo, the experiment is called a blind study.

It is possible that experimenters can unwittingly influence results by knowing which subjects are receiving which treatment. Therefore, in a double blind study, even the experimenters do not know if they are delivering the placebo or the drug. Although the experimental approach is a powerful tool for examining causality, researchers must avoid errors that can lead to faulty conclusions.

Tests

Psychologists develop and use specialized tests to measure many types of variables. For example, personality tests, which assess personality traits, often contain questions that ask how a person typically feels or behaves. Other psychological tests consist of performance tasks. For example, intelligence tests may ask people to assemble objects or solve arithmetic problems. Neuropsychological tests help diagnose normal and abnormal brain functioning by measuring how people perform mental and physical tasks, such as recalling lists of words or manipulating objects.

To enhance learning and chances of performing well on tests, one can apply scientific psychological principles regarding time management, strategies for studying more effectively, test preparation strategies, and techniques for taking tests.

Statistical Methods

Statistics are woven into the fabric of modern life, and they are integral to psychological research. Typically it is difficult to make sense out of the data collected by examining the individual score of each participant. Descriptive statistics allow us to summarize and describe the characteristics of a set or distribution of data.

Descriptive- Two types of descriptive statistics are measures of central tendency and measures of variability.

   a) **Measures of Central Tendency-** Given a set of data, measures of central tendency address the question "What is the typical score?" One measure, the mode, is the most frequently occurring score in a distribution. A second measure is the median, the point that divides a distribution of scores in half when those scores are arranged in order from lowest to highest. Finally, the mean is the arithmetic average of a set of scores. Because the mean takes all the information in a set of scores into account, it is the most commonly used measure of central tendency.

   b) **Measures of Variability-** To describe a set of data, researchers want to know, not only the typical score, but also whether the scores cluster together or vary widely. Measures of variability capture the degree of variation or spread in a distribution of scores. The simplest but least informative measurement is the range, which is the difference between the highest and lowest scores in a distribution. A more important statistic is the standard deviation which takes into account how much each score in a distribution differs from the mean.

Inferential- Descriptive statistics allow researchers to efficiently summarize data, but researchers typically want to go beyond mere description and draw inferences (conclusions) from their data. Inferential statistics tell us how confident one can be in making inferences about a population, based on findings obtained from a sample.

   a) **Null Hypothesis-** A null hypothesis is a hypothesis that proposes no relationship or difference between two variables.

   b) **Alternative Hypothesis-** Proposes a relationship between two or more variables.

c) **Statistical Significance-** Means that it is very unlikely that a particular finding occurred by chance alone. Psychologists typically consider results to be statistically significant only if the results could have occurred by chance alone in fewer than 5 times in 100.

Psychological Specialties

Psychology is the scientific study of behavior and the mind. The term 'behavior' refers to actions and responses that we can directly observe, whereas the term 'mind' refers to internal states and processes, such as thoughts and feelings that cannot be seen directly and that must be inferred from observable, measurable responses. Because psychologists study biological, psychological, and environmental factors that affect a wide array of behaviors, psychological science intersects with many other disciplines; and many subfields and areas of specialty have developed.

- **Clinical Psychology-** The study and treatment of mental disorders. Many clinical psychologists diagnose and treat people with psychological problems in clinics, hospitals, and private practice. Some are also scientists who conduct research on the causes of mental disorders and the effectiveness of various treatments.
- **Biopsychology-** Focuses on the biological underpinnings of behavior, examining how the brain processes, genes, and hormones influence our actions, thoughts, and feelings.
- **Developmental Psychology-** Examines human physical, psychological, and social development across the life span.
- **Experimental Psychology-** Focuses on basic processes such as learning, sensory systems, perception, and motivational states. Most research in this field involves laboratory experiments, often with nonhuman animals.
- **Industrial-organizational Psychology-** Examines people's behavior in the workplace.
- **Psychometrician-** Practices the science of measurement, or psychometrics. The term psychometrics refers to the measurement of an individual's psychological attributes, including the knowledge, skills, and abilities a professional might need to work in a particular job or profession.
- **Personality Psychology-** Focuses on the study of human personality.
  Social Psychology- Examines people's thoughts, feelings, and behavior pertaining to the social world. Studies how people influence each other, behave in groups, and form impressions and attitudes.

Science involves both basic research, which reflects the quest for knowledge for its own sake, and applied research, which is designed to solve specific, practical problems. For psychologists, most basic research examines how and why people behave, think, and feel the way they do. In applied research, psychologists often use basic scientific knowledge to design interventions.

Modern psychologists work in many settings. They teach, conduct research, perform therapy and counseling, and apply psychological principles to enhance human welfare and help shape public policy.

Unit One Practice Quiz

1. Which branch of psychology seeks to examine behaviors and thoughts pertaining to the workplace?
   A) Social psychology
   B) Clinical psychology
   C) Industrial-organizational psychology
   D) Developmental psychology

2. True or False: Inferential statistics describes a set of data including measures of central tendency.
   A) True
   B) False

3. Marcy wishes to ask all of the students in a high school about their drinking habits. Which method of research should she pursue in order to get effective and efficient data?
   A) Survey
   B) Naturalistic observation
   C) Experiment
   D) Case study

4. Which hypothesis states that there is no relationship between the independent and dependent variable?
   A) Alternative hypothesis
   B) Null hypothesis

5. Which perspective of psychology emphasizes free will and personal growth?
   A) Evolutionary psychology
   B) Social psychology
   C) Developmental psychology
   D) Humanistic psychology

6. B.F. Skinner was one of the leading pioneers in research for:
   A) Behaviorism
   B) Classical conditioning
   C) Psychodynamic training
   D) Gestalt psychology

7. True or False: An animal behaviorist may use naturalistic observation to record data about a species in their undisturbed habitat.
   A) True
   B) False

8. All of the following research methods are feasible for studying large groups EXCEPT:

A) Survey
B) Experiment
C) Case study
D) Longitudinal study

Answer Key: 1=C, 2=B, 3=A, 4=B, 5=D, 6=A, 7=A, 8=C

Unit Two: Biological Influences on Behavior

Learning Objectives
After completing Unit Two, you will be able to:

1. Describe the biological bases of behavior, by discussing the impact of genetic influences on behavior
2. Describe the impact of evolution on behavior, utilizing five evolution theories and their impact on behavior
3. Discuss environmental influences on behavior
4. Describe the influence of hormones on behavior
5. Describe the hierarchical brain structures and behavioral functions

Genes, Evolution, and Environment
Humans have wondered how physical characteristics are transmitted from parents to their offspring. Many have wondered how genetics influence behavior and how people adapt to their environment.

Genetic Influences
Early in the 20th century, geneticists made the important distinction between genotype (the specific genetic makeup of the individual), and phenotype (the individual's observable characteristics).

a) **Genes and Heritability**
1. **Individual Differences**- At a biological level, genes direct the process of development by programming the formation of protein molecules, which can vary in infinite ways. Heredity potential is carried in the genes and genotype is present from conception.
2. **Group Differences**- Phenotype can be affected by both genes and the environment. Genetic structure and phenotype are not identical, in part because some genes are dominate while others are recessive and many characteristics are influenced by the interactions of multiple genes.

b) **DNA**
The egg cell from the mother and the sperm cell from the father carry within their nuclei the material of heredity, in the form of rod like units called chromosomes. A chromosome is a double stranded and tightly coiled molecule of DNA. All of the information for heredity is encoded in the combinations of four chemical bases - adenine, thymine, guanine, and cytosine - that occur throughout the chromosome. Within each DNA molecule, the sequence of the four letters of the DNA alphabet - A, T, G, C - creates the specific commands for every feature and function of the person.

The DNA portion of the chromosome body carries the genes, the biological units of heredity. With the exception of the egg and sperm cells, every cell in the body carries within its nucleus 23 pairs of chromosomes, each containing numerous genes that regulate every aspect of cellular functioning. Every cell nucleus in the body contains the genetic code for the entire body.

- c) **Genome**

    In 1990, geneticists began the Human Genome Project, a coordinated effort to map DNA, including all the genes, of the human organism. The genetic structure in every one of the 23 chromosome pairs has now been mapped, by methods that allow investigators to literally disassemble the genes in each chromosome and study their specific sequences of bases (A,T,G, and C). The first results of the genome project showed that the human genome consists of approximately 25,000 genes; and the location and structure of more than 80 genes that contribute to hereditary diseases have been identified through gene mapping.

Evolution

The separate paths of behaviorism and ethology have increasingly converged, reminding us that the environment shapes behavior in two fundamental ways: through species adaptation and through personal adaptation. Our personal adaptation to life's circumstances occurs through the laws of learning, resulting from our interactions with immediate and past environments. The environment also influences species adaptation. Over the course of evolution, the environmental conditions faced by each species helped shape biology. Theorists proposed that, as the human brain evolved, it acquired capacities that enhanced our ability to learn and solve problems. Evolution is a change over time in the frequency with which particular genes, and the characteristics they produce, occur within an interbreeding population.

- a) **Charles Darwin-** He was an English naturalist and geologist, best known for his contributions to evolutionary theory. He established that all species of life descended over time from common ancestors. He introduced the scientific theory that this branching pattern of evolution resulted from a process that he called natural selection, in which the struggle for existence has a similar effect as the artificial selection involved in selective breeding.

- b) **Natural Selection-** Characteristics that increase the likelihood of survival and reproduction within a particular environment are more likely to be preserved in the population, and therefore become more common in the species over time. As environmental changes produce new and different demands, various new characteristics may contribute to survival and the ability to pass on one's genes. In this way, natural selection acts as a set of filters, allowing certain characteristics of survivors to become more common.

c) **Instincts/Mental Modules-** Darwin's theory of evolution inspired many early psychological views that instincts motivate much of our behavior. An instinct is an inherited characteristic, common to all members of a species that automatically produces a particular response when the organism is exposed to a particular stimulus. To evolutionary psychologists, what we call human nature is the expression of inborn biological tendencies that have evolved through natural selection.

d) **Universal Traits-** Culture plays an important role in shaping our present and past experiences, and strongly affects how we learn. Cultural socialization influences our beliefs and perceptions, our social behavior, our sense of identity, the skills we acquire, and countless other characteristics. Learning is the mechanism through which the environment exerts its most profound effects on behavior.

e) **Courtship and Mating-** The only way to continue the species is through reproduction. In order to pass on one's genes and maintain the species, people must mate. One of the most important and intimate ways that humans relate to one another is by seeking a mate. Marriage seems to be universal across the globe. In seeking mates, women and men display different mating strategies and preferences. According to an evolutionary viewpoint, called sexual strategies theory, mating strategies and preferences reflect inherited tendencies, shaped over the ages in response to the different types of adaptive problems that men and women faced. Another theory, referred to as the social structure theory, maintains that men and women display different mating preferences, not because nature impels them to do so, but because society guides them into different social roles.

Environmental Influences

Nature vs. Nurture
Behavior geneticists study how genetic and environmental factors contribute to the development of psychological traits and behaviors. Adoption and twin studies are the major research methods used to disentangle hereditary and environmental factors. The environment exerts its effects largely through learning processes, made possible by innate biological mechanisms. Humans and other animals can learn which stimuli are important and which responses are likely to result in goal attainment, thereby allowing them to regulate their behavior and adapt to the environment.

a) **Personality-** Personality has a strong genetic contribution, though not as strong as that for intelligence. Shared family environment seems to have little impact on the development of personality traits. Unshared individual experiences are far more important environmental determinates.

b) **Intelligence-** Intelligence has a strong genetic basis, with the individual inheriting a range for potential intelligence that has upper and lower limits measured through IQ testing. Environmental effects will then determine where the person falls within these genetically determined boundaries.

Nervous System

The evolutionary history of our species, the genes inherited from parents, and life experiences have shaped us. From a psychological perspective, the most important physical organ is the brain. To understand how the brain controls experience and behavior, we must first understand how its individual cells function, and how they communicate with one another.

Neurons- Neurons are the basic building blocks of the nervous system and are the pathways for communication. They are also referred to as nerve cells.

  a) **Components of the Neuron-** Each neuron has three main parts: a cell body, dendrites, and an axon. The cell body, or soma, contains the biochemical structures needed to keep the neuron alive, and its nucleus carries the genetic information that determines how the cell develops and functions. Emerging from the cell are branch-like fibers, called dendrites, which are specialized receiving units like antennae that collect messages from neighboring neurons and send them on to the cell body. There, the incoming information is combined and processed. All parts of a neuron are covered by a protective membrane that controls the exchange of chemical substances between the inside and outside of the cell. These exchanges play a critical role in the electrical activities of nerve cells. Extending from one side of the cell body is a single axon, which conducts electrical impulses away from the cell body to other neurons, muscles, or glands. Many axons that transmit information throughout the brain and spinal cord are covered by a tube-like myelin sheath, a whitish fatty insulation layer which accelerates the transmission of information.

  b) **Synapse-** The parts of a single neuron are physically connected, so electrical signals are able to travel from one end of the neuron to the other without interruptions. Between neurons, however, is a small gap. The junctions where the end of one neuron meets the beginning of another is called a synapse and the gap between them is called the synaptic gap. Communication across this gap is accomplished with neurotransmitters, rather than with electrical impulses.

  c) **Nerve Impulse-** Neurons do their work through the use of electrical impulses and neurotransmitters. A signal (information) from a sense receptor or another neuron, coming in through a neuron's dendrites, gets passed along when it triggers an action potential, or electrical impulse, that travels down the axon and then triggers activity in whichever neurons, muscles, or glands join up with the axon. Neurons do two important things. Like tiny batteries, they generate electricity that creates nerve impulses. They also release chemicals that allow them to communicate with other neurons and muscles and glands. At rest, the neuron has an electrical resting potential due to the distribution of positively and negatively charged chemical ions inside and outside of the neuron. When stimulated, a flow of ions in and out through the cell membrane reverses the electrical charge of the resting potential, producing an action potential, or nerve impulse. The original ionic balance is restored, and the neuron is again at rest.

Neurotransmitters- Are chemical molecules contained in vesicles, or sacs, within the axon terminal. When an action potential, or electrical impulse arrives at the terminal, the neurotransmitters are released into the synaptic cleft. They then bind to receptor sites on the next neuron's dendrites. The neurotransmitters are chemical substances that carry messages across the synaptic space to the other neurons, muscles, or glands. Different neurotransmitters affect different neurons. Because different neural pathways are made up of different neurons and have different functions, each neurotransmitter affects behavior differently.

Endorphins- Most neurotransmitters have their excitatory and inhibitory effects only on specific neurons that have receptors for them. Others, called neuromodulators, have a more widespread and generalized influence on synaptic transmission. These substances circulate through the brain and either increase or decrease the sensitivity of neurons to their specific transmitters. The best known neuromodulators are the endorphins, which travel through the brain's circulatory system and inhibit pain transmission, while enhancing neural activity that produces pleasurable feelings.

Central Nervous System- The central nervous system includes the brain, which controls many physiological and psychological functions, and the spinal cord, which enables reflexive behavior and relays information to the brain from elsewhere in the body.

Brain- Neuroscientists use four different methods to study the brain's structures and activities, through various research methods.

   a. **Research Methods-** Because of scientific and technical advances, more has been learned about the brain in the past four decades than was known throughout the preceding ages.

   - **Neuropsychological Tests-** Psychologists have developed a variety of neuropsychological tests to measure verbal and nonverbal behaviors of people who have suffered brain damage through accident or disease. The Trial Making Test is used to assess brain function, testing memory and planning. Scores on the test give an indication of the type and severity of brain damage. The tests are also used to assess learning disabilities and developmental disorders.

   - **Destruction and Stimulation Techniques-** Experimental studies are another useful method of learning about the brain. In this method, researchers chemically or electrically stimulate the neurons. In chemical stimulations, a tiny tube, or cannula, is inserted into a precise area of the brain so that chemicals, including neurotransmitters, can be delivered directly and their effects on behavior studied. A specific region of the brain can also be stimulated by a mild electric current.

- **Electrical Recording-** Because electrodes can record brain activity as well as stimulate it, scientists can measure the activity of large groups of neurons through a series of large electrodes placed on the scalp. This method is known as electroencephalography (EEG). Clinicians use the EEG to detect abnormal electrical patterns that signal the presence of brain pathology.

- **Brain Imaging-** The newest tools of discovery are imaging techniques that permit neuroscientists to look into the living brain. A CT scan (computerized axil tomography) uses x-ray techniques to study brain structures. A MRI (magnetic resonance imaging) creates images based on how atoms in living tissue respond to a magnetic pulse delivered by the device. Whereas CT scans and MRIs provide pictures of brain structures, PET scans (positron-emission tomography) measure brain activity, including metabolism, blood flow, and neurotransmitter activity.

- **Split-brain-** The visual system's anatomy made studies of split-brain subjects possible. Images entering the eye are reversed by the lens. This led to the development of simple ways to test the functions of two hemispheres after the corpus callosum was cut and the patients had recovered from their surgery. The results showed that in some ways the operation had created two minds in one body. The results of split-brain research were so dramatic that they led some people to promote the concept of brain functions as being highly localized and restricted to one hemisphere or the other.

b. **Hemispheres-** The brain is divided structurally into the hindbrain, the midbrain, and the forebrain. This organization reflects the evolution of increasingly complex brain structures related to behavioral capabilities.

- **Hindbrain-** The hindbrain is the lowest and most primitive level of the brain. As the spinal cord enters the brain, it enlarges to form the structures that compose the stalk-like brain stem. Attached to the brain stem is the other major portion of the hindbrain, the cerebellum.

- **Midbrain-** Lying just above the hindbrain, the midbrain contains clusters of sensory and motor neurons. The sensory portion of the midbrain contains important relay centers for the visual and auditory systems. Here, nerve impulses from the eyes and ears are organized and sent to the forebrain structures involved in visual and auditory perception. The midbrain also contains motor neurons that control eye movement.

- **Forebrain-** The forebrain is the brain's most advanced portion, from an evolutionary standpoint. Its major structure, the cerebrum, consists of two large hemispheres, a left side and a right side, that wrap around the brain stem. The outer portion of the forebrain has a thin covering, or cortex. Within are a number of important structures buried in the central regions of the hemispheres. The two cerebral hemispheres work in coordination with each other, and they appear to have different functions and abilities. The left hemisphere commands language and mathematical abilities; and positive emotions are linked to the left side. The right hemisphere controls spatial abilities but has a generally limited ability to communicate through speech; and negative emotions are linked to the right side of the brain. The brain normally operates as a highly integrated system.

c. **Parts of the Brain-**The structures of the brain's core, which we share with all other vertebrates, govern the basic physiological functions that keep us alive, such as breathing and heart rate. Built upon these basic structures are newer systems that involve progressively more complex functions - sensing, wanting, thinking, and reasoning.

- **Cortex-** The cerebral cortex, a ¼ inch thick sheet of gray unmyelinated cells that form the outermost layer of the human brain, is the crowning achievement of brain evolution, and in humans constitutes 80 percent of brain tissue. The cerebral cortex is divided into the frontal, parietal, occipital, and temporal lobes. Some areas of the cerebral cortex receive sensory input, some control motor functions, and others (the association cortex) are involved in higher mental processes in humans. The frontal lobes are particularly important in such executive functions as planning, voluntary behavior, and self-awareness, perception, language, and thought.

- **Medulla-**The 1.5 inch medulla is the first structure above the spinal cord and plays an important role in vital body functions such as heart rate and respiration. Because of the medulla, these functions occur automatically. Damage to the medulla can result in death, or at best, the need to be maintained on a life support system. The medulla is also a two-way thoroughfare for all the sensory and motor nerve tracts coming up from the spinal cord and descending from the brain. Most of these tracts cross over within the medulla, so the left side of the brain receives sensory input from and exerts motor control over the right side of the body, and the right side of the brain serves the left side of the body.

- **Corpus Callosum-** The left and right hemispheres are connected by a broad white band of myelinated nerve fibers. The corpus callosum is a neutral bridge consisting of white myelinated fibers which act as a major communication link between the two hemispheres and allow them to function as a single unit.

- **Pons-** A word meaning bridge in Latin, lies just above the medulla and carries nerve impulses between higher and lower levels of the nervous system. The pons has clusters of neurons that help regulate sleep. Like the medulla, the pons helps control vital functions, especially respiration, and damage to it can produce death.

- **Reticular Formation-** Buried within the midbrain is a finger-shaped structure that extends from the hindbrain up into the lower portions of the forebrain. The reticular formation acts as a kind of sentry, both alerting higher centers of the brain that messages are coming and then either blocking those messages or allowing them to go forward. The reticular formation plays a vital role in consciousness, attention, and sleep. Activity of the ascending reticular formation excites higher areas of the brain and prepares them to respond to stimulation. The descending reticular formation acts as a gate, determining which stimuli enter into consciousness.

- **Cerebellum-** Attached to the rear of the brain stem is the little brain known as the cerebellum. Its wrinkled cortex or covering, consists mainly of gray cell bodies (gray matter). The cerebellum is concerned primarily with muscular movement coordination, but it also plays a role in learning and memory.

d. **Limbic System-** The limbic system is a set of structures lying deep within the cerebral hemispheres. The limbic system helps coordinate behaviors needed to satisfy motivational and emotional urges that arise in the hypothalamus. It also is involved in memory.

- **Thalamus-** The thalamus is located above the midbrain and resembles two small footballs, one within each cerebral hemisphere. The thalamus has sometimes been likened to a switchboard that organizes inputs from sensory organs and routes them to the appropriate areas of the brain. The visual, auditory, and the body senses all have major relay stations in the thalamus.

- **Hypothalamus-** Which means literally under the thalamus, consists of a tiny group of neuron cell bodies that lie at the base of the brain, above the roof of the mouth. The hypothalamus plays a major role in many aspects of motivation and emotion, including sexual behavior, temperature regulation, sleeping, eating, drinking, and aggression. The hypothalamus has an important connection with the endocrine system and through its connection with the pituitary gland, it regulates sexual development and sexual behavior, metabolism, and reactions to stress.

- **Hippocampus-** One key structure of the limbic system is the hippocampus, which is involved in forming and retrieving memories. Damage to this area can result in severe short-term memory impairment.

- **Amygdala-** Another key structure of the limbic system, the amygdala organizes motivational and emotional response patterns, particularly those linked to aggression and fear. The amygdala is a key part of a larger control system for anger and fear that also involves other brain regions.

e. **Lobes-** Each of the two hemispheres (left and right) of the cerebral cortex is divided into four regions, each having a variety of functions.

- **Occipital-** Located at the base of the skull, in the back, the occipital lobes are involved in vision.

- **Frontal-** Located just behind the forehead, the frontal lobe plays a part in coordinating movement and in higher level thinking such as planning and predicting the consequences of behaviors. They are also involved in speech: Broca's area, located in the frontal lobe, is mainly involved in the production of speech through its connections with the motor cortex region that controls the muscles used in speech.

- **Parietal-** Located at the top of the head, behind the frontal lobes, the parietal lobes are involved in the sense of touch, among other things, and allow us to keep tabs on where our hands and feet are and what they are up to.

- **Temporal-** Located on either side of the ears, the temporal lobes are involved in hearing. Another important area located in the temporal lobe is Wernicke's area which is primarily involved in speech comprehension.

f. **Spinal Cord-** The spinal cord contains sensory neurons and motor neurons. Interneurons inside the spinal cord serve a connective function between the two. Simple stimulus response sequences can occur as spinal reflexes. The central nervous system includes the brain, which of course controls many physiological and psychological functions, and the spinal cord, which enables reflective behavior and relays information to the brain from elsewhere in the body.

g. **Peripheral Nervous System-** The peripheral nervous system contains all the neural structures that lie outside of the brain and the spinal cord. Its specialized neurons help carry out both the input functions that enable us to sense what is going on inside and outside our bodies, and the output functions that enable us to respond with our muscles and glands. The peripheral nervous system has two major divisions, the somatic nervous system and the autonomic nervous system.

- **Somatic Nervous System-** Consists of sensory neurons that are specialized to transmit messages from the eyes, ears, and other sensory receptors, and the motor neurons that send messages from the brain and spinal cord to the muscles that control voluntary movements. The somatic nervous system carries information from muscles, sense organs, and skin to the central nervous system, allowing the sensations of pressure, pain, and temperature, among other things. It also carries messages from the central nervous system to skeletal muscles, allowing for voluntary movement.

- **Autonomic Nervous System-** The body's internal environment is regulated largely through the activities of the autonomic nervous system. The autonomic nervous system senses the body's internal functions, and it controls the glands and the smooth (involuntary) muscles that form the heart, the blood vessels, and the lining of the stomach and intestines. The autonomic nervous system is largely concerned with involuntary functions, such as respiration, circulation, and digestion; it is involved in many aspects of motivation, emotional behavior, and stress responses. It consists of two subdivisions, the sympathetic and the parasympathetic nervous system.

    i. **Sympathetic Nervous System-** Has an activation or arousal function, and it tends to act as a total unit. The sympathetic nervous system prepares the body for action, also referred to as the fight-or-flight mode. Responses include quickening of the heart rate, widening of the arteries, and stimulation of the sweat glands.

    ii. **Parasympathetic Nervous System-** Deactivates the systems mobilized by the sympathetic nervous system and is in operation during states of relaxation. Responses include decreased heart rate, breathing rate, and digestive functioning.

h. **Hormones-** The endocrine system secretes hormones into the blood stream. These chemical messengers affect many bodily processes, including those associated with the central and autonomic nervous system.

- **Melatonin-** This hormone is secreted by the pineal gland, has a relaxing effect on the body and promotes a readiness for sleep.

- **Oxytocin-** Is a pituitary hormone that stimulates uterine contractions during childbirth and triggers lactation.

- **Adrenal hormones-** The adrenal glands are twin structures perched atop the kidneys and serve as hormone factories producing and secreting about 50 different hormones that regulate many metabolic processes within the brain and other parts of the body. The adrenals produce the neurotransmitter dopamine, as well as several stress hormones. In an emergency, the adrenal glands are activated by the sympathetic branch of the autonomic nervous system. Stress hormones are then secreted into the bloodstream, mobilizing the body's emergency response system.

- **Sex Hormones-** Are commonly considered to be testosterone, estrogen, and progesterone. Testosterone is often referred to as a "male" hormone, and estrogen and progesterone are often referred to as "female" hormones.

Unit Two Practice Quiz

1. What is the name of the hormone responsible for inducing sleepiness in mammals?
   A) Adrenaline
   B) Melatonin
   C) Dopamine
   D) Estrogen

2. True or False: The smallest piece of genetic unit is called the genome.
   A) True
   B) False

3. The _____ is the part of the limbic system involved in forming and retrieving memories.
   A) Thalamus
   B) Amygdala
   C) Hypothalamus
   D) Hippocampus

4. True or False: Oxytocin is a key hormone in stimulating contractions during childbirth.
   A) True
   B) False

5. Which lobe of the brain is located at the rear of the skull?
   A) Occipital
   B) Parietal
   C) Temporal
   D) Frontal

6. Which part of the brain is responsible for the "fight-or-flight" response to fear?
   A) Pons
   B) Cerebellum
   C) Amygdala
   D) Hippocampus

7. True or False: The parasympathetic nervous system controls the fight/flight arousal function.
   A) True
   B) False

8. All of the following are building blocks of DNA EXCEPT:
   A) Adenine
   B) Guanine
   C) Cytosine
   D) Thiamin

Answer Key: 1=B, 2=B, 3=D, 4=A, 5=A, 6=C, 7=B, 8=D

Unit Three: Sensation and Perception

Learning Objectives
After completing this unit, you should be able to:

1. Discuss the area of psychophysics and the process in which our sense organs receive and transmit information
2. Discuss the sensory systems including vision, auditory, taste, and smell and their involvement in receiving and transmitting information
3. Discuss how the body perceives touch, pain, body position, and other sensations
4. Discuss how the brain interprets sensory input
5. Discuss what underlies our perceptions of the physical world

Psychophysics and Thresholds
Psychophysics is the area of psychology that addresses the topic of sensation: the levels of intensity at which we can detect stimuli, how sensitive we are to changes in stimulation, and how psychological factors influence our ability to sense stimuli. According to signal detection theory, our ability to notice a stimulus will vary due to psychological factors including motivation, past experiences, and expectations.

In some ways, sensation and perception blend together making it difficult to separate the two. Nevertheless, psychologists do distinguish between them. **Sensation** is the stimulus detection process by which our sense organs respond to and translate environmental stimuli into nerve impulses that are sent to the brain. **Perception** is making sense of what our senses tell us. It is the active process of organizing this stimulus input and giving it meaning. The minimum stimulation needed for a given person to detect a given stimulus (an odor, taste, sound, etc.) is called an absolute threshold. It is typically thought of as the intensity necessary for a stimulus to be detected 50 percent of the time that it is presented. The smallest difference a person can detect between two similar stimuli is called the just noticeable difference or the difference threshold. According to Weber's Law, this threshold increases in proportion to the intensity and magnitude of the stimuli.

Sensory Adaptation
From a survival perspective, it is important to know when some new development requires our attention. Sensory neurons are engineered to respond to a constant stimulus by decreasing their activity, and the diminishing sensitivity to an unchanging stimulus is called sensory adaptation. Sensory adaptation is adaptive, because it frees our senses from the constant and the mundane, allowing them to pick up informative changes in the environment that could be important to our well-being or survival.

Vision

a) **The Visual Stimulus-** The normal stimulus for vision is electromagnetic energy, or light waves, which are measured in nanometers (nm), or one billionth of a meter. Light-sensitive visual receptor cells are located in the retina. The rods are brightness receptors, and the less numerous cones are color receptors. Light energy striking the retina is converted into nerve impulses by chemical reactions in the photo pigments of the rods and cones. Visual stimuli are analyzed by feature detectors in the primary visual cortex, and the stimulus elements are restructured and interpreted in light of input from the visual association cortex.

b) **The Eye Structure and Function-** Light waves enter the eye through **cornea,** a transparent protective structure at the front of the eye. Behind the cornea is the **pupil,** an adjustable opening that can dilate or constrict to control the amount of light that enters the eye. The pupil's size is controlled by muscles in the colored **iris** that surrounds the pupil. Behind the pupil is the **lens**, an elastic structure that becomes thinner to focus on distant objects and thicker to focus on nearby objects. The lens of the eye focuses the visual image on the **retina**, a multilayered light sensitive tissue at the rear of the fluid filled eyeball. The retina contains two types of light sensitive receptor cells called rods and cones. Rods are found throughout the retina except in the **fovea,** a small area in the center of the retina that contains no rods but many densely packed cones. Rods and cones send their messages to the brain via two additional layers of cells. The rods and cones have synaptic connections with a thin layer of ganglion cells, whose axons are collected into a bundle to form the **optic nerve**.

c) **Color Vision-** Around 1800 it was discovered that any color in the visible spectrum can be produced by some combination of the wavelengths that correspond to the colors blue, green and red. This theory is referred to as the trichromatic theory.

The second influential theory is the opponent-process theory which proposes that each of the three cone types responds to two different wavelengths. One type responds to blue or yellow, another to red or green, and a third to black or white. In essence, color vision is a two-stage process having both trichromatic and opponent-process components.

Hearing

a) **Auditory Stimulus-** The stimuli for our sense of hearing are sound waves, a form of mechanical energy. What we call sound is actually pressure waves in the air, water, or some other conducting medium. Sound waves have two characteristics: frequency, measured in terms of cycles per second or hertz (Hz); and amplitude, measured in terms of decibels (dB). Frequency is related to pitch, amplitude to loudness. Loudness is coded in terms of the number and types of auditory nerve fibers that fire. Pitch is coded in two ways. According to the frequency of pitch perception, nerve impulses sent to the brain match the frequency of the sound wave. The other theory, known as the place theory of pitch perception, suggests that the specific point in the cochlea where the fluid wave peaks and most strongly bends the hair cells, serves as a frequency coding cue.

   b) **The Ear Structure and Function-** The transduction system of the ear is made up of tiny bones, membranes, and liquid-filled tubes designed to translate pressure waves into nerve impulses. At a speed of about 75 mph, sound waves travel into an auditory canal leading to the **eardrum**, a membrane that vibrates in response to sound waves. Beyond the eardrum is the **middle ear**, a cavity housing three tiny bones. The vibrating activity of these bones - the **hammer** (malleus), **anvil** (incus), and the **stirrup** (stapes) - amplifies the sound waves more than 30 times. The **oval window** forms the boundary between the middle ear and the inner ear. The inner ear contains the <u>cochlea</u>, a coiled snail-shaped tube that is filled with fluid and contains the **basilar membrane**, a sheet of tissue that runs its length. Resting on the basilar membrane is the **organ of Corti**, which contains about 16,000 tiny hair cells that are the actual sound receptors. The tips of the hair cells are attached to another membrane, **the tectorial membrane.**

   When sound waves strike the eardrum, pressure created at the oval window by the hammer, anvil, and stirrup of the middle ear sets the fluid inside the cochlea into motion. The fluid waves that result vibrate the basilar membrane and the tectorial membrane, causing bending of the hair cells in the organ of Corti. This bending of the hair cells triggers the release of neurotransmitters into the synaptic space between the hair cells and the neurons of the auditory nerve, resulting in nerve impulses being sent to the brain.

Taste

Gustation is the sense of taste which is a chemical sense. Our sense of taste responds to only four qualities: sweet, sour, salty, and bitter. Every other taste experiment combines these qualities and those of other senses, such as smell, temperature, and touch. Taste buds are chemical receptors concentrated along the tip, edges, and back surface of the tongue. An additional taste sensation, called umami, increases the intensity of other taste qualities.

Smell

Olfaction is the sense of smell. The receptors for smell are long cells that project through the lining of the upper part of the nasal cavity and into the mucous membrane. Olfactory receptors fire, sending their input to the olfactory bulb, a forebrain structure immediately above the nasal cavity. Each odorous chemical excites only a limited portion of the olfactory bulb, and odors are apparently related perceptions, statements or coded in terms of the specific area of the olfactory bulb that is excited.

Skin Senses

The skin and body senses include the sense of touch, kinesthesis (muscle movement), and equilibrium. The last two are called body senses because they inform us of the body's position and movement.

   a) **Touch and Temperature-** Touch is important to us in many ways. Sensitivity to extreme temperatures and to pain enables us to escape external danger and alerts us to disorders within our body. Humans are sensitive to at least four tactile sensations: pressure (touch), pain, warmth, and cold. These sensations are conveyed by receptors in the skin and in our internal organs. Mixtures of these four sensations form the basis for all other common skin sensations. The primary receptors for pain and temperature are the free nerve endings, simple nerve cells beneath the skin's surface that resemble bare tree branches. Basket cell fibers situated at the base of hair follicles are receptors for touch and light pressure. Kinesthesis functions by means of nerve endings in the muscles, tendons, and joints. The sense organs for equilibrium are in the vestibular apparatus of the inner ear.

   b) **Pain-** Pain receptors are found in all body tissues with the exception of the brain, bones, hair, nails, and nonliving parts of the teeth. Free nerve endings in the skin and internal organs respond to intense mechanical, thermal, or chemical stimulation. They then send nerve impulses into the spinal cord, where sensory tracts carry information about pain intensity and location to the thalamus. The thalamus relays the information to the somatosensory and frontal areas of the cerebral cortex. Other tracts from the thalamus direct nerve impulses to the limbic system, which is involved in motivation and emotion. Thus pain has both a sensory and an emotional component.

   The Gate Control theory proposes that the experience of pain results from the opening and closing of gating mechanisms in the nervous system. The nervous system has its own built in analgesics of pain impulses from the spinal cord to the brain with opiate-like properties. The natural opiates are called endorphins and exert some sort of pain killing effect by inhibiting the release of neurotransmitters involved in the synaptic transmission.

Basic Perceptual Phenomena

To create our perceptions, the brain carries out two different processing functions. In bottom-up processing, the system takes in individual elements of the stimulus and combines them into a unified perception. In top-down processing, sensory information is interpreted in light of existing knowledge, concepts, ideas, and expectations. The perception of movement is a complex process, sometimes requiring the brain to integrate information from several different sources.

a) **Patterns-** Recognizing a stimulus implies that we have a perceptual schema - a mental representation or image containing the critical and distinctive features of a person, object, event, or other perceptual phenomenon.

b) **Constancies-** Allow us to recognize familiar stimuli under varying conditions. In vision, several constancies are important. Shape constancy allows us to recognize people and other objects from many different angles. Brightness constancy is where the relative brightness of objects remains the same under different conditions of illumination. Size constancy is the perception that the size of objects remains relatively constant, even though images on our retina change in size with variations in distance.

c) **Depth Perception-** The retina receives information in only two dimensions (length and width), but the brain translates these cues into three-dimensional perceptions. It does this by using both monocular depth cues, which require only one eye, and binocular depth cues, which require both eyes. Monocular cues to judge distance and depth include patterns of light and shadow, linear perspective, interposition, height in the horizontal plane, texture, clarity, relative size, and motion parallax. Binocular disparity occurs as slightly different images are viewed by each eye and acted on by feature detectors for depth. A second binocular distance cue, convergence, is produced by feedback from the muscles that turn eyes inward to view a close object.

d) **Gestalt Principles of Organization-** Gestalt psychologists were among the first to formulate rules by which the brain pieces together meaningful experiences out of fragments of sensation. The Gestalt theorists emphasized the importance of **figure-ground relations**, our tendency to organize stimuli into a central or foreground figure and a background. Gestalt theorists were interested in how separate stimuli come to be perceived as parts of larger wholes. The **law of proximity** says that elements near each other are likely to be perceived as belonging together. The **law of similarity** says that when parts of a configuration are perceived as similar, they will be perceived as belonging together. In the **law of closure**, people tend to close the open edges of a figure or fill gaps in an incomplete figure, so that their identification of form is more complete than it actually is. Finally, the **law of continuity** holds that people link individual elements together, so that they form a continuous line or pattern that makes sense.

e) **Illusions-** Our analysis of perceptual schemas, hypotheses, and constancies allows us to understand some interesting perceptual experiences known as illusions, that is, compelling but incorrect perceptions. Such perceptions can be understood as erroneous perceptual hypotheses about the nature of a stimulus.

Influences on Perception

Perceptual development involves both physical maturation and learning. Some perceptual abilities are innate or develop shortly after birth, whereas others require particular experiences early in life in order to develop. Cultural factors can influence certain aspects of perception, including picture perception and susceptibility to illusions. However, many aspects of perception seem constant across cultures. Visual deprivation studies, manipulation of visual input, and studies of restored vision have shown that the normal biological development of the perceptual system depends on certain sensory experiences at early periods of development.

Subliminal Perception

Not all stimuli register in awareness. A subliminal stimulus is one that is so weak or brief that, although it is received by the senses, it cannot be perceived consciously. Although subliminal stimuli cannot control consumer behavior, research suggests that such stimuli do affect more subtle phenomena such as perceptions and behavior.

Extrasensory Perception

ESP is most commonly called the "sixth sense." It is sensory information that an individual receives beyond the ordinary five senses of sight, hearing, smell, taste, and touch. It can provide the individual with information of the present, past, and future; as it seems to originate in a second, or alternate reality. The term "ESP" was used in 1870 by Sir Richard Burton. A French researcher, Dr. Paul Joire used the term ESP in 1892 to describe the ability of person who had been hypnotized or was in a trance state to externally sense things without using their ordinary senses.

The argument rests on the hypothesis that two realities exist, the physical one and a second one. ESP can occur when there is an integration between both realities. This occurs infrequently and only when the barriers between the realities are broken. It does not happen often, because if it did, all unconscious thought would flood and overflow the conscious mind, a condition which the mind could not withstand.

Unit Three Practice Quiz

1. Which of the following is NOT a taste sensation?
   A) Sweet
   B) Bitter
   C) Olfactory
   D) Salty

2. True or False: The cochlea forms the boundary between the middle and inner ear.
   A) True
   B) False

3. The _____ theory states that pain is controlled by the opening and closing of nerve channels.
   A) Gate Control
   B) Pain Control
   C) Olfactory Control
   D) Kinethesis Control

4. True or False: ESP is also known as the "sixth sense", or extra sensory perception.
   A) True
   B) False

5. Which form of depth perception involves combining images from both eyes?
   A) Occipital
   B) Binocular
   C) Monocular
   D) Retinal

6. Which Gestalt law states that elements that are near each other are likely to be perceived as belonging together?
   A) Proximity
   B) Closure
   C) Continuity
   D) Similarity

7. True or False: Illusions are images that the brain forms that actually exist.
   A) True
   B) False

8. Which Gestalt theory states that we have a tendency to categorize images into a foreground and background?
   A) Closure
   B) Reciprocity
   C) Figure-Ground Relations
   D) Gate Control

Answer Key: 1=C, 2=B, 3=A, 4=A, 5=B, 6=A, 7=B, 8=C

Unit Four: Consciousness

Learning Objectives
After completing this unit, you should be able to:

1. Discuss the characteristics of consciousness
2. Discuss circadian rhythms and biological rhythm, REM sleep and dreaming
3. Discuss different types of sleep disorders
4. Discuss hypnosis states and theories of hypnosis
5. Discuss the physical and psychological effects of psychoactive drugs and the different classes of drugs

Biological Rhythms

In psychology, consciousness is often defined as our moment to moment awareness of ourselves and our environment. Consciousness is: subjective and private; dynamic and ever changing; self-reflective and central to our sense of self; and intimately linked to selective attention. Selective attention is the process that focuses awareness on some stimuli to the exclusion of others.

In humans and other species, hormone levels, body temperature, and wakefulness rise and fall in predictable ways during the course of a day. These are known as circadian rhythms. Circadian rhythms are 24-hour biological cycles that help regulate bodily processes and influence our alertness. Most circadian rhythms are regulated by the brain's suprachiasmatic nuclei (SCN), located in the hypothalamus, and known as the master circadian clock. Free running circadian rhythms are about hours. The day-night cycle and other environmental factors reset our daily clocks to a 24-hour cycle.

Circadian rhythms influence our tendency to be a morning or a night person. Cultural factors may also play a role. In general, our alertness is lowest in the early morning hours. Job performance errors, major industrial accidents, and fatal auto accidents peak during these hours. Jet lag, night shift work, and seasonal affective disorder involve circadian disruptions. Treatments include controlling one's exposure to light, taking oral melatonin, and regulating one's daily activity schedule.

Sleep

Circadian rhythms promote a readiness for sleep by decreasing alertness, but they do not regulate sleep directly. Roughly every 90 minutes while asleep, we cycle through different stages in which brain activity and other physiological responses change in a generally predictable way. As sleep begins, our brain wave patterns become more irregular.

    a) **Stages of Sleep-** Sleep has five main stages. **Stage one** is a light sleep from which we can easily awaken. We spend just a few minutes in this stage, often characterized by vivid images, sudden body jerks, and occasional dreams. **Stage two** is characterized by sleep spindles, which are periodic 1-2 second bursts of rapid brain wave activity. Muscles are much more relaxed, breathing and heart rate are slower, dreams may occur and it is harder to awaken. As **stage three** begins, the brain starts to produce delta waves which appear on an EEG monitor as large, slow waves. Stage 3 is a transition into **stage four**, which involves stronger, more consistent delta waves. These two stages together are referred to as slow-wave sleep, last about 30 minutes, and are the most difficult from which to awaken.

b) **REM Sleep and Dreaming-** About an hour after falling asleep, individuals begin to move back into stage 3 and then stage 2. But instead of sliding back into stage 1, people typically move into a 10-minute period of REM (rapid eye movement) sleep. In REM, brain waves are similar to stage 1, but breathing is more rapid and irregular, the heart rate increases, and the eyes dart back and forth underneath closed eyelids. It is usually during REM sleep that people dream. These dreams are prevented from being acted out because the brainstem blocks messages from the motor cortex, which leaves the body more or less paralyzed. REM sleep is, in fact, sometimes called paradoxical sleep, because the sleeper appears calm and relaxed despite a great deal of cortical activity. After the REM stage, the sleeper moves back into stage 2 and the next cycle continues. With each cycle, however, periods of REM sleep become longer and periods of stage 4 sleep become shorter.

Freud saw dreams as a way to preserve sleep. He suggested that the manifest content of the dream (the images that actually appear to the dreamer) was a disguised version of the dream's latent content (usually a forbidden sexual or aggressive urge that the dreamer would repress if awake). By distorting or disguising the wish, the dreamer avoids the anxiety that would accompany his awareness of it, and therefore, can remain asleep. According to the activation-synthesis theory, the brain's neurons fire randomly during sleep, and as we awaken, we construct a dream in order to make sense out of the random images that have been generated. The information processing theory claims that dreams are a way to consolidate information. As we dream we sort through the day's events and stamp them into memory.

c) **Functions of Sleep-** According to the restoration model, sleep recharges our run down bodies and allows us to recover from physical and mental fatigue. Evolutionary/circadian sleep models emphasize that sleep's main purpose is to increase a species' chance of survival in relation to its environmental demands. Activation-synthesis theory views dreaming as the brain's attempt to fit a story to a random neural activity.

d) **Sleep Disorders-** Several sleep disorders can interfere with typical sleep patterns. **Insomnia** refers to chronic difficulty falling asleep, or experiencing restful sleep. **Narcolepsy** involves extreme daytime sleepiness and sudden, uncontrollable sleep attacks that may last from less than a minute to an hour. **REM-sleep behavior**

disorder (RBD) is where the loss of muscle tone that causes normal REM sleep paralysis is absent. **Night terrors** are frightening dreams that arouse the sleeper to a near panic state. **Nightmares** are bad dreams and virtually everyone has them. **Sleep apnea** is repeatedly stopping and restarting to breathe during sleep. **Sleep walking** usually occurs during the stage 3 or 4 period of slow wave sleep. Sleepwalkers often stare blankly and are unresponsive to other people.

Hypnosis

Hypnosis is an induced state of consciousness characterized by deep relaxation and heightened suggestibility. However, there is no evidence that someone who is hypnotized will do things he or she wouldn't do if he/she were not under hypnosis. Hypnosis is a procedure in which one person (the subject) is guided by another (the hypnotist) to respond to suggestions for changes in subjective experience, alterations in perceptions, sensation, emotion, thought, or behavior.

   a) **Hypnotic Phenomena-** Hypnotic induction is a process that creates a context for hypnosis, and hypnotized people subjectively experience their actions to be involuntary. Hypnosis can have striking physiological effects. For patients who experience chronic pain, hypnosis can produce relief that lasts for months or even years. Brain imaging research reveals that hypnosis modifies neural activity in the brain areas that process painful stimuli. Non-hypnotic techniques, such as imagery and performing distracting cognitive tasks, also alter neural functioning and reduce pain. Some people can be led to experience hypnotic amnesia (during the session itself) and posthypnotic amnesia (after coming out of hypnosis). Hypnosis increases the risk that people will develop distorted memories about events in response to leading questions.

   b) **Theories of Hypnosis-** Dissociation theories view hypnosis as an altered state of divided consciousness. Social-cognitive theory states that hypnotic experiences occur because individuals have strong expectations about hypnosis and are highly motivated to take on the role of being hypnotized.

Psychoactive Drugs

Psychoactive drugs produce a state of consciousness that is different from normal consciousness by mimicking, inhibiting, or stimulating the activity of neurotransmitters.

   a) **Physiology of Drug Effects-** Drugs enter the bloodstream and are carried throughout the brain by small blood vessels called capillaries. Capillaries contain a blood-brain barrier, a special lining of tightly packed cells that lets vital nutrients pass through so that neurons can function. The blood-brain barrier screens out many foreign substances, but some, including various drugs, can pass through. Once inside, they alter consciousness by facilitating or inhibiting synaptic transmission.

Neurotransmitters are synthesized inside presynaptic (sending) neurons and stored in vesicles. Next, they are released into the synaptic space, where they bind with and stimulate receptor sites on postsynaptic (receiving neurons). Finally, neurotransmitter molecules are deactivated by enzymes. An agonist is a drug that increases the activity of a neurotransmitter. An antagonist is a drug that inhibits or decreases the action of a neurotransmitter.

b) **Psychology of Drug Effects-** When a drug is used repeatedly, the intensity of effects produced by the same dosage level may decrease over time. The decreasing response to a drug is called tolerance. As it develops, a person must take increasingly larger doses to achieve the same physical or psychological effects. Tolerance develops when the body produces compensatory responses to counteract a drug's effect. When drug use is stopped, compensatory responses continue and produce withdrawal symptoms. Drug addiction, which is formally called substance dependence, is a maladaptive pattern of substance use that causes a person significant distress or substantially impairs that person's life. A drug's effect depends on its chemical actions, the physical and social setting, cultural norms and learning, and the user's genetic predisposition, expectations, and personality.

c) **Classes of Drugs-** Stimulants, such as amphetamines, cocaine, and ecstasy, increase arousal, body functions, and boost mood. Depressants, such as alcohol, barbiturates, and tranquilizers, decrease neural activity and slow down body functions. Opiates increase endorphin activity, producing pain relief and mood changes and are highly addictive. Hallucinogens powerfully distort sensory experience and can blur the line between reality and fantasy. Marijuana produces relaxation at low doses, but can cause anxiety and sensory distortions at higher dosages. It can also impair thinking and reflexes.

Unit Four Practice Quiz

1. Casey has trouble falling asleep and staying asleep. She might have a condition known as:
   A) Insomnia
   B) Narcolepsy
   C) RBD
   D) Night terrors

2. True or False: Stage IV is the lightest form of sleep.
   A) True
   B) False

3. How many hours long is the human circadian rhythm?
   A) 12 hours
   B) 6 hours
   C) 8 hours
   D) 24 hours

4. Which category of drugs decreases neural and physical activity?
   A) Stimulants
   B) Depressants

5. What stage of sleep includes sleep spindles?
   A) I
   B) II
   C) III
   D) IV

6. Which sleep disorder is characterized by a cycle of stopping and restarting of breathing?
   A) Sleep walking
   B) Night terrors
   C) Narcolepsy
   D) Sleep apnea

7. True or False: An agonist is a drug that decreases the action of a neurotransmitter.
   A) True
   B) False

8. All of the following are examples of depressants EXCEPT:
   A) Marijuana
   B) Alcohol
   C) Caffeine
   D) Barbiturates

Answer Key: 1=A, 2=B, 3=D, 4=B, 5=B, 6=D, 7=B, 8=C

Unit Five: Learning and Memory

Learning Objectives
After completing this unit, you should be able to:

1. Discuss the how the concepts of learning and adaptation are related
2. Discuss the key principles and applications of operant conditioning
3. Discuss the key elements and applications of observational learning
4. Discuss how we encode information into memory
5. Discuss how we retrieve memories and what factors make memory retrieval easier

Learning
Learning is a process in which experience produces a relatively enduring change in an organism's behavior or capabilities. Think of learning as how the predictability of events can change behavior. Experience can be thought of as earlier events that influence the way an organism behaves in the present. Traditionally, that meant studying the effects of experiences with various stimuli on an organism's behavior. (Any factor in the environment that causes a reaction is known as a stimulus, and any reaction by an organism, either voluntary or involuntary, is called a response.)

Classical Conditioning
This is a learning process that involves pairing a neutral stimulus with an unconditioned stimulus. An organism learns to associate the two stimuli, so that one stimulus comes to elicit a response that originally was elicited only by the other stimulus. This particular type of learning by association is also called Pavlovian conditioning.

   a) **Unconditioned Stimulus (UCS) -** A stimulus that elicits a reflexive or innate response (UCR) without prior learning.

   b) **Unconditioned Response (UCR) -** A reflexive or innate response that is elicited by a stimulus (the UCS) without prior learning.

   c) **Conditioned Stimulus (CS) -** A stimulus that, through association with a UCS, comes to elicit a conditioned response similar to the original UCR.

   d) **Conditioned response (CR) -** A response elicited by a conditioned stimulus.

Classical conditioning involves the learning of an association between two stimuli. It involves pairing a neutral stimulus with an unconditioned stimulus (UCS) that elicits an unconditioned response (UCR). Through pairing, the neutral stimulus becomes a conditioned stimulus (CS) that evokes a conditioned response (CR) similar to the original unconditioned response (UCR).

Acquisition refers to the period of time during which a response is being learned and involves conditioned stimulus and unconditioned stimulus pairings. Extinction represents the disappearance of the conditioned response when the conditioned stimulus is presented repeatedly without the unconditioned stimulus. After, extinction, spontaneous recovery of the conditioned response may occur when the controlled stimulus is presented after a rest period.

Bodily and psychological responses can be classically conditioned, including fears, sexual attraction, positive and negative attitudes, nausea, and immune system responses. Techniques based on classical conditioning are highly successful in treating phobias.

Operant Conditioning

Is a type of learning in which behavior is influenced by the consequences that follow. Learning the association between behavior and consequences either increases or decreases the frequency of the behavior / response, depending on the quality of the consequence. Thorndike's law of effect states that responses followed by satisfying consequences are strengthened, whereas those followed by annoying consequences are weakened. Skinner analyzed operant conditioning in terms of antecedents, behaviors, and consequences.

Discriminative stimuli are antecedents that signal the likely consequences of particular behaviors in a given situation.

Reinforcement

Reinforcement occurs when a response is strengthened by its consequences, which always involve something pleasant. It is also accompanied by an increase in the target behavior. The words "positive" and "negative" refer to the type of stimulus.

a) **Positive Reinforcement-** A response is strengthened by the subsequent presentation of a stimulus that feels good.

b) **Negative Reinforcement-** A response is strengthened by the removal of an aversive stimulus.

c) **Primary Reinforcement-** Are stimuli such as food and water, that an organism naturally finds reinforcing because they satisfy biological needs.

d) **Secondary Reinforcement-** Stimuli that acquire reinforcing properties through their association with primary reinforcers.

Punishment

Punishment occurs when a response is weakened by its consequences, which always involve something unpleasant. It is also accompanied by a decrease in target behavior.

a) **Positive Punishment-** Also referred to as aversive punishment or punishment by application, where a response is weakened by the subsequent presentation of an unpleasant stimulus, and can produce rapid results.

b) **Negative Punishment-** Also referred to as punishment by removal or response cost, where a response is weakened by the subsequent removal of a pleasant stimulus.

c) **Consequences-** In general a consequence that occurs immediately after a behavior has a stronger effect than one that is delayed. Training animals typically requires immediate reinforcement so that they associate the correct response. Because humans can imagine future consequences, our behavior is less rigidly controlled by the timing of consequences.

Schedules of Reinforcement

In daily life, reinforcement comes in different patterns and frequencies. These patterns, called schedules of reinforcement, have strong and predictable effects on learning, extinction, and performance.

a) **Continuous Reinforcement-** Is a process by which every response of a particular type is reinforced. This process produces more rapid learning because the association of a behavior and its consequences is easier to perceive.

b) **Intermittent Reinforcement-** Also referred to as partial reinforcement, is a process in which only a portion of the responses of a particular type are reinforced. This process produces behavior that is learned more slowly but is more resistant to extinction.

c) **Generalization-** In operant conditioning, stimulus generalization is the tendency to respond to a new stimulus as if it is the original discriminative stimulus. Here stimuli similar to the initial conditioned stimulus elicit a conditioned response.

d) **Discrimination-** A discriminative stimulus is a cue that indicates the kind of consequence that is likely to occur after a response. In operant conditioning, stimulus discrimination is the tendency for a response to happen only when a particular stimulus is present. This is demonstrated when a conditioned response occurs to one stimulus but not to others.

e) **Extinction-** Is a process in which the conditioned stimulus is presented repeatedly in the absence of the unconditioned stimulus, causing the conditioned response to weaken and eventually disappear. In operant conditioning it is the gradual disappearance of a response when it stops being reinforced.

f) **Spontaneous Recovery-** Is the reappearance of a previously extinguished conditioned response after a rest period and without new learning traits.

g) **Behavior Modification-** Operant conditioning research gave rise to a field called applied behavior analysis, which combines a behavioral approach with the scientific method to solve individual and societal problems. Essentially applied behavior analysts design and implement a program to change behavior, and they measure its effectiveness objectively by gathering data before and after the program is in place. The procedures that are used to change behavior are collectively known as behavior modification.

h) **Observational Learning-** Is the process by which learning occurs by observing the behavior of a model. This type of learning can be highly adaptive. By observing others, an organism can learn which events are important, which stimuli signal that such events are about to occur, and which responses are likely to produce positive or negative consequences. Humans' capacity to learn by observation, which is also called modeling, far exceeds other creatures. Bandura's social-cognitive theory, also known by its former name social-learning theory, emphasizes that people learn by observing the behavior of models and acquiring the belief that they can produce behaviors to influence events in their lives.

Memory
Memory refers to the processes that allow us to record, store, and later retrieve experiences and information. Memory adds richness and context to our lives, but even more fundamentally, it allows us to learn from experience and thus adapt to changing environments.

Memory as a Reconstructive Process
Retrieving information from long-term memory is not like viewing a digital replay. Our memories are often incomplete or sketchy. We may literally construct or reconstruct a memory by piecing together bits of stored information in a way that seems real and accurate.

a) **Eyewitness Testimony-** If memories are constructed then information that occurs after an event may shape that construction process. This misinformation effect is known as the distortion of a memory by misleading post-event information. Even one or two words can produce a misinformation effect while questioning an eyewitness.

Misinformation effects also occur because of source confusion, also called source monitoring error; our tendency to recall something or recognize it as familiar but to forget where we encountered it. Vulnerability to misinformation effects is greater among younger than older children, and when suggestive questions are asked repeatedly. Experts cannot reliably tell when children are reporting accurate memories versus sincerely believed false memories. Psychologists debate whether or not recovered memories of child abuse are accurate, and whether or not the abuse was forgotten through repression or other psychological processes. Concern about the possibility of false memory leads many experts to urge caution in unconditionally accepting the validity of recovered memories.

b) **Flashbulb Memories-** Retrieval cues activate information stored in long-term memory. Retrieval is more likely when we have multiple, self-generated, and distinctive cues. We experience flashbulb memories as vivid snapshots of events and are confident of their accuracy. Over time, flashbulb memories may become inaccurate. Overall, memory accuracy and confidence are weakly to moderately related.

c) **Confabulation-** Confabulation is a memory disorder that causes people to have inaccurate memories. These inaccuracies may range from distortion of minor details, to complete fabrication of the entire memory. The disorder is known to be caused by brain damage, such as from an aneurysm, or by dementia, such as Alzheimer's disease. People who confabulate are not lying, they have no intention to deceive, and they are not even aware that they are giving wrong information.

Stages of Memory- Memory is typically divided into three types: sensory, short-term, and long-term, and involves three main processes: encoding, storage, and retrieval.

a) **Sensory-** Sensory memory briefly holds incoming sensory information and is fleeting awareness of whatever the senses have detected. Some of this information reaches the short-term memory and long-term memory, where it is mentally represented by visual, phonological, semantic, or motor codes.

b) **Short-term-** Short-term memory is also called working memory because it stores information that can be kept in the mind long enough to solve problems. Working memory processes a limited amount of information and supports other cognitive functions. It has phonological, visuospatial, episodic, and executive components.

c) **Long-term-** Long-term memory stores large amounts of information for up to a lifetime. It is unlimited and perhaps acts as a permanent storehouse of memories.

Memory Aids- Storing information is useless, without the ability to retrieve it. A retrieval cue is a stimulus, whether internal or external, that activates information stored in long-term memory.

   a) **Encoding-** Refers to getting information into the system by translating it into a neural code that the brain processes. This is a little like what happens when typing on a computer keyboard. Our ability to retrieve a memory is influenced, not only by the nature of the original stimulus, but also by environmental, physiological, and psychological factors. The encoding specificity principle states that memory is enhanced when the cues present during retrieval match the cues present during encoding. These cues may involve the same environment (context dependent memory) or same internal state (state dependent memory) present during original encoding.

   b) **Rehearsal-** According to the concept of levels of processing, the more deeply we process information, the better we remember it. Rehearsal goes beyond mere exposure. When we rehearse information, we are thinking about it. Maintenance rehearsal involves simple, rote repetition and keeps information active in working memory. Elaborative rehearsal involves focusing on the meaning of information or expanding and elaborating on it in some way. Elaborative rehearsal provides a deeper processing than maintenance rehearsal.

   c) **Mnemonic Devices-** This is a form of a memory aid that reorganizes information into more meaningful units and provide extra clues to help retrieve information from long-term memory. Organizing material in a hierarchy takes advantage of the principle that memory is enhanced by associations between concepts. A logical hierarchy enhances our understanding of how individual items are related. Chunking refers to combining individual items into larger units of meaning. Dual coding theory means encoding information using both verbal associations and visual imagery, because the odds improve that at least one of the codes will be available later to support recall. The method of loci is a memory aid that associates information with mental images of physical locations.

Forgetting- We often cannot recall information because we never encoded it into long-term memory in the first place.

   a) **Decay Theory-** Proposes that with time and disuse, the long-term physical memory trace in the nervous system fades away.

   b) **Replacement Theory-** Holds that new information entering the memory replaces old information already stored.

   c) **Interference-** According to this theory, we forget information because other items in long-term memory impair our ability to retrieve it. Proactive interference occurs when material learned in the past interferes with recall of newer material. Retroactive interference occurs when newly acquired information interferes with the ability to recall information learned at an earlier time.

d) **Repression-** Is a motivational process that protects us by blocking the conscious recall of anxiety arousing memories.

e) **Cue dependent-** Is the failure to recall information without memory cues, along with the failure to recall a memory due to missing stimuli or cues that were present at the time the memory was encoded.

Unit Five Practice Quiz

1. In classical conditioning, an unlearned, inborn reaction to a stimulus is known as a(n):
   A) Conditioned response
   B) Unconditioned response
   C) Conditioned stimulus
   D) Unconditioned stimulus

2. True or False: Confabulations are distortions of memories that appear to be real to the user.
   A) True
   B) False

3. Learning that results from punishments or rewards of certain behaviors are known as:
   A) Classical conditioning
   B) Punishment learning
   C) Gate control
   D) Operant conditioning

4. Which part of the memory acts as a permanent and unlimited storehouse?
   A) Short-term
   B) Long-term

5. Reinforcers that are inherently comforting, such as water and food, are known as:
   A) Primary
   B) Primal
   C) Secondary
   D) Tertiary

6. George repeats his grocery list multiple times in order to store it in his short-term memory. This mnemonic device is also known as:
   A) Displacement
   B) Coding
   C) Rehearsal
   D) Replacement

7. True or False: Spontaneous recovery is the sudden disappearance of a learned behavior.
   A) True
   B) False

8. Patrice shocks her dog every time he enters the bedroom. Eventually, he learns to stop entering the bedroom. Patrice used _____:
   A) Positive reinforcement
   B) Positive punishment

C) Negative reinforcement
D) Negative punishment

Answer Key: 1=B, 2=A, 3=D, 4=B, 5=A, 6=C, 7=B, 8=B

Unit Six: Motivation and Emotion

Learning Objectives
After completing this unit, you should be able to:

1. Discuss how motives function in our lives and how our diverse motives influence behavior
2. Describe what happens when motives conflict with one another
3. Discuss how biological factors influence our behaviors
4. Discuss how psychological factors influence our behaviors
5. Discuss how environmental factors influence behaviors
6. Discuss how culture influences emotional experiences and expression

Specific Motives
The concept of motivation is central in our attempt to understand behavior and its causes. Motivation is defined as a process that influences the direction, persistence, and vigor of goal-directed behavior. Motivation can be defined as the psychological process that energizes and directs behavior.

Hunger- Is often used to illustrate how factors can impact the occurrence and expression of a motive. Many theoretical perspectives address the topic of motivation and provide insight into the nature, functions, and consequences of motivation.

a) **Genetics and Set-point-** Darwin's theory of evolution inspired the early psychological views that instincts motivate our behavior. An **instinct** (also called a fixed action pattern) is an inherited characteristic, common to all members of a species that automatically produces a particular response when the organism is exposed to a particular stimulus. Modern evolutionary psychologists propose that many human motives have evolutionary underpinnings expressed through the actions of genes. **Homeostatic models** view motivation as an attempt to maintain equilibrium in bodily functions. **Drive theories** propose that tissue deficits create drives, such as hunger, that push a organism to reduce that deficit and restore homeostasis. **Psychological processes** attempt to keep the body in energy homeostasis. Changes in the supply of glucose available to cells provide one signal that helps initiate hunger. Many researchers believe that there is a **set point**, a biologically determined standard around which body weight (or more accurately, fat mass) is regulated. This view holds that if we overeat or undereat, homeostatic mechanisms alter our energy utilization and hunger drive so as to restore the body's set point.

b) **Influences of Gender and Culture-** Incentives represent environmental stimuli that pull an organism toward a goal. Through classical conditioning, neutral stimuli can acquire the capacity to trigger hunger. Cultural norms affect our food preferences and eating habits. Heredity and the environment affect our susceptibility to becoming obese.

Attitudes, habits, and psychological needs regulate food intake. Especially for women, food restriction often stems from social pressures to conform to cultural standards of beauty. Women have become increasingly dissatisfied with their body image throughout the last half of the 20th century. Overall, men's perceptions serve to keep them satisfied with their figures, whereas women's perceptions place pressure on them to lose weight.

c) **Eating Disorders-** Anorexia and bulimia occur more often in cultures that value thinness, and are associated with somewhat different psychological profiles. Heredity predisposes some people to developing eating disorders. Victims of anorexia nervosa have an intense fear of being fat and severely restrict their food intake to the point of self-starvation. People who suffer from bulimia nervosa are also afraid of becoming fat, and they binge eat and then purge the food, usually by inducing vomiting or using laxatives. Anorexia and bulimia are more common in industrialized cultures were thinness is equated with beauty. Personality factors associated with people who have anorexia show these people to be perfectionists and high achievers. Those with bulimia tend to be depressed and anxious, exhibit low impulse control, and seem to lack a stable sense of personal identity.

d) **Obesity-** Is often blamed on a lack of willpower, a dysfunctional way of coping with stress, heightened sensitivity to external food cues and emotional disturbances. Heredity influences one's basal metabolic rate and the tendency to store energy as either fat or lean tissue. Overall, genetic factors appear to account for about 40-70 percent of the variation in BMI among women and men. More than 200 genes have been identified as possible contributors to human obesity. The environment also affects our susceptibility to obesity including the following factors: an abundance of inexpensive, tasty foods that are high in fat and carbohydrates; a cultural emphasis on getting the best value which contributes to supersizing menu items; and technological advances that decrease the need for daily physical activity.

Love and Sex- The motive for sex is often described as biological reproductive, yet people usually do not have sex to conceive children. In reality, people engage in sex to reproduce, obtain and give sensual pleasure, express love, foster intimacy, fulfill a "duty," conform to peer pressure, and for a host of other reasons.

a) **Attachment-** The past half century has witnessed changing patterns of sexual activity, such as an increase in premarital sex, which now appears to have leveled off. In general, single adults who cohabit (are not married but live with a sexual partner) are the most sexually active, followed by married adults. Single adults who do not cohabit are the least active.

b) **Biological Influences-** During sexual intercourse, people often experience a four stage physiological response pattern, consisting of excitement, plateau, orgasm, and resolution. During the **excitement phase**, arousal builds rapidly and blood flow increases to arteries in and around the genital organs. In the **plateau phase**, arousal continues to build until there is enough muscle tension to trigger an orgasm. During the **orgasm phase** in males, rhythmic contractions of internal organs and muscle tissue surrounding the urethra project semen out of the penis. In females, there are rhythmic contractions of the outer third of the vagina and surrounding muscles. In males, orgasm is ordinarily followed by **a resolution phase**, during which physiological arousal decreases rapidly and the genital organs return to their normal condition. As with hunger, the hypothalamus plays a key role in sexual motivation. It controls the pituitary gland, which regulates the secretion of hormones, called gonadotropins, into the bloodstream. Sex hormones have organizational effects that direct the development of male and female sex characteristics. Sex hormones also have activational effects that stimulate sexual desire and behavior.

c) **Psychological Influences-** Environmental stimuli affect sexual desire. Viewing sexual violence reinforces men's belief in rape myths and generally increases men's aggression toward women. Sexual orientation involves dimensions of self-identity, sexual attraction, and actual sexual behavior. Scientists still do not completely understand the basis for sexual orientation. Psychological factors can not only trigger sexual arousal but also inhibit it. Sexual dysfunction refers to chronic impaired sexual functioning that distresses a person. It may result from injuries, diseases, and drug effects, but in some cases it may be psychological. Anyone who doubts culture's power to shape human behavior need only examine sexual customs around the globe; and the psychological meaning of sex itself depends on cultural contexts.

Achievement- The need for achievement is a positive desire to accomplish tasks and compete successfully with standards of excellence. High need achievers have a strong motive for success and relatively low fear of failure. They tend to seek moderately difficult tasks that are challenging but attainable. Low need achievers are more likely to choose easy tasks, where success is assured, or very difficult tasks, where success is **expected**.

a) **Achievement Goal Theory-** Focuses on the manner in which success is defined both by the individual and within the achievement situation itself. At the individual level, achievement goal theorists are interested in the achievement goal orientation that people have. They differentiate between a **mastery orientation**, in which the focus is on personal improvement, giving maximum effort, and perfecting new skills, and an **ego orientation**, in which the goal is to outperform others (hopefully, with as little effort as possible). At the situational level, the theory focuses on the **motivational climate** that encourages or rewards either a mastery approach or an ego approach.

b) **Achievement Goal Orientations-** Another way to understand achievement motivation is to examine the goals that people seek to attain in task situations. **Mastery approach goals** focus on the desire to master a task and learn new knowledge and skills. **Ego approach goals** reflect a competitive orientation that focuses on outperforming other people.

c) **Avoidance-** On the avoidance side, **mastery avoidance goals** reflect a fear of not performing up to one's own standards. **Ego-avoidance goals** center on avoiding being outperformed by others. Compared with ego-involving environments, mastery-involving motivational climates foster more positive psychological and performance outcomes. Motivational goals may conflict with one another. **Approach-approach conflict** occurs when a person has to select between two attractive alternatives, whereas **avoidance-avoidance conflict** involves choosing between two undesirable alternatives. **Approach-avoidance** conflict occurs when we are attracted to and repelled by the same goal.

d) **Self-efficacy-** The belief that one is capable of carrying out the specific behaviors needed to attain one's goals. When people are successful and when they attribute their success to their own competencies, their self-efficacy increases and assists then in subsequent goal-directed efforts.

Maslow and Hierarchy of Needs- Abraham Maslow proposed that needs exist in a hierarchy, from basic biological needs to the ultimate need for self-actualization. After our basic physiological needs are satisfied, we focus on our need for safety and security. Once that is met, we then attend to needs at the next higher level, and so on. If situations change and lower-level needs are no longer met, we refocus our attention on them until they are satisfied.

To Maslow, self-actualization, which represents the need to fulfill our potential, is the ultimate human motive. It motivates us to perfect ourselves mentally, artistically, emotionally, and socially, to explore activities for their intrinsic satisfaction rather than to gain esteem and belongingness, and to live deep and meaningful lives dedicated to the betterment of all people, not just ourselves. Maslow believed that most people become so focused on attaining satisfaction of the needs lower in the hierarchy (**physiological needs**- food, drink, **safety needs**- security and psychological safety, **belongingness**- acceptance and affection, **esteem**- approval and recognition, **self-actualization**), that they spend little time focused on becoming all they can be. Those rare people who approach self-actualization achieve a state of self-transcendence, moving beyond a focus on self to commit themselves to the welfare of others, to spiritual fulfillment, and to causes higher than themselves.

Emotions- Are feeling (or affect) states that involve a pattern of cognitive, physiological, and behavioral reactions to events. Emotions prepare us to deal with the many ways in which events can impact our motives, goals, and values. Emotions have important adaptive functions. Emotions are also an important form of social communication. By providing clues about our internal states and intentions, emotions influence how other people behave toward us. Positive emotions are an important part of life satisfaction, and negative emotions foster unhappiness.

Our emotional states share four common features: emotions are triggered by external or internal **eliciting stimuli**; emotional responses result from our **appraisals** of these stimuli, which give the situation its perceived meaning and significance; our **bodies respond physiologically** to our appraisals; and emotions include **behavior tendencies,** either **expressive behaviors** or **instrumental behaviors**, ways of doing something about the stimulus that evoked the emotion.

Physiology of Emotions- When our feelings are stirred up, one of the first things we notice is bodily changes. Many parts of the body are involved in emotional arousal, but certain brain regions, the autonomic nervous system, and the endocrine system play especially significant roles.

a) **Face-** Many parts of the body can communicate feelings, but we tend to concentrate on what the face tells us. Although we can never directly experience another person's feelings, we often can infer that someone is angry, sad, fearful, or happy on the basis of expressive behaviors, the person's observable emotional displays.

b) **Brain-** Emotions involve important interactions between several brain areas, including the limbic system and cerebral cortex. Our physiological responses in emotion are produced by the hypothalamus, the limbic system, the cortex, and the autonomic and endocrine systems. There appear to be two systems for emotional behavior, one involving conscious processing by the cortex and the other involving unconscious processing by the amygdala. Negative emotions seem to reflect greater relative activation of the right hemisphere, whereas positive emotions are related to relatively greater activation in the left hemisphere.

c) **Role of Hormones-** The fight-or-flight response is produced by the sympathetic branch of the autonomic nervous system and by hormones from the endocrine system. The sympathetic nervous system produces arousal within a few seconds by directly stimulating the organs and muscles of the body. Meanwhile, the endocrine system pumps epinephrine, cortisol, and other stress hormones into the bloodstream.

d) **Deception and the Polygraph-** A scientific instrument known as a polygraph measures physiological responses, such as respiration, heart rate, and skin conductance (which increases in the presence of emotion due to sweat gland activity). Because we have less control over physiological responses than over numerous other behaviors, many people regard the polygraph as a nearly infallible means of establishing whether or not someone is telling the truth. The validity of the polygraph as a lie detector has been questioned, largely because of the difficulty of establishing the meaning of recorded physiological responses.

Cultural Influences- Certain gestures, body postures, and physical movements can convey vastly different meanings in different cultures.

   a) **Display Rules-** Cultural display rules dictate when and how particular emotions are to be expressed. Many emotional theorists conclude that innate biological factors and cultural display rules combine to shape emotional expression across different cultures.

   b) **Body Language-** Emotional responses are often calls to action, requiring a response to the situation that aroused the emotion. These are instrumental behaviors directed at achieving some emotional relevant goal. There is an optimal level of arousal for the performance of any task. The optimal level varies with the complexity of the task; complex tasks have lower optimal levels. The **James-Lange theory** maintains that we first become aroused and then judge what we are feeling. The **Cannon-Bard** theory proposes that arousal and cognition are independent and simultaneously triggered by the by the thalamus. According to **Lazarus's cognitive-affective theory**, appraisals trigger emotional arousal; in contrast, according to Schachter's two-factor theory of emotion, arousal tells us how strongly we are feeling while cognitions derived from situational cues helps us label the specific emotion.

Unit Six Practice Quiz

1. Which goal theory focuses on the desire to outperform other people?
   A) Mastery approach
   B) Approach-approach
   C) Ego approach
   D) Approach-avoidance

2. True or False: Bulimia nervosa involves binging and purging in order to lose weight.
   A) True
   B) False

3. Which of the following is NOT an example of an instrumental behavior?
   A) Eating healthy to lose weight
   B) Practicing the guitar to play well
   C) Yelling when angry
   D) Ripping up a picture to get over somebody

4. True or False: Self-actualization is the top tier of Maslow's hierarchy of needs.
   A) True
   B) False

5. This tier of Maslow's hierarchy involves a need for approval and recognition:
   A) Physiological
   B) Self-actualization
   C) Esteem
   D) Belongingness

6. Which of the following is a facial expression of fear?
   A) Smiling
   B) Heart rate increase
   C) Slow blinking
   D) Widening of the eyes

7. True or False: Display rules are cultural depictions of how emotions are to be expressed.
   A) True
   B) False

8. Which of the following is the first stage of the human sexual response pattern?
   A) Orgasm
   B) Excitement
   C) Plateau
   D) Resolution

Answer Key: 1=C, 2=A, 3=C, 4=A, 5=C, 6=D, 7=A, 8=B

Unit Seven: Thinking and Intelligence

Learning Objectives
After completing this unit, you should be able to:

1. Discuss how we reason and make decisions
2. Discuss the elements of cognition
3. Discuss how cognitive biases affect problem solving
4. Discuss the nature of intelligence
5. Discuss heredity, culture, and environment and how they shape intelligence
6. Discuss the nature of IQ testing.

Cognition- Can be thought of as the mental activities involved in solving problems: thinking, language, memory, and intelligence. A variety of thought processes either facilitate or impede problem solving.

Elements of Cognition- Much of our thinking occurs in the form of propositions, statements that express ideas. All propositions consist of concepts combined in a particular way.
   a) **Concepts-** Are basic units of semantic memory - mental categories into which we place objects, activities, abstractions, and events that have essential features in common.

   b) **Prototypes-** Many concepts are defined by prototypes, the most typical and familiar members of a category or class.

   c) **Schema-** Is a mental framework, an organized pattern of thought about some aspect of the world. Concepts and categories represent types of schemas, and together they help us build a mental framework of our world.

Thinking and Consciousness- Thinking seems to be the internal language of the mind and includes several mental activities. One mode of thought takes the form of verbal statements that we make in our minds. This is called **propositional thought** because it expresses a proposition or statement. Another mode, **imaginal thought**, consists of images that we can see, hear, or feel in our mind. A third mode, **motoric thought**, is related to mental representations of motor movements, such as throwing an object.

The **conscious mind** is our awareness at the present moment. The **subconscious mind** consists of accessible information. We become aware of this information once we direct our attention to it. Think of this as memory recall. The **unconscious mind** consists of primitive, instinctual wishes, as well as inaccessible information. Although our behaviors might indicate the unconscious forces that drive them, we don't have easy access to the information stored in the unconscious mind. During our childhood, we acquired countless memories and experiences that formed who we are today. However, we cannot recall most of those memories. They are unconscious forces (beliefs, patterns, subjective maps of reality) that drive our behaviors.

Types of Reasoning- Reasoning is one aspect of intelligent thinking. It helps us acquire knowledge, make sound decisions, solve problems, and avoid the hazards and time-consuming efforts of trial and error.

a) **Deductive Reasoning-** Reasoning from the top down, that is, from general principles to a conclusion about a specific case. When people reason deductively, they begin with a set of premises and determine what the premises imply about a specific situation. Deductive reasoning is the basis of formal mathematics and logic.

b) **Inductive Reasoning-** Reasoning from the bottom up, starting with specific facts and trying to develop a general principle. Inductive reasoning leads to likelihood rather than certainty.

c) **Algorithmic-** Formulas are precise sequences of procedures that automatically generate solutions. Mathematical formulas are algorithms and if used properly will always give the correct answer.

d) **Heuristics-** Are general problem-solving strategies, similar to mental rules of thumb that we apply to certain classes of situations. One common heuristic, **means-ends analysis**, involves identifying differences between the present situation and a desired goal, and making changes that reduce these differences. Another heuristic, **subgoal analysis,** involves formulating subgoals, or intermediate steps, toward a solution. **Representativeness heuristic** involves thinking about how closely something fits our prototype for that particular concept, or class, and therefore how likely it is to be a member of that class.

e) **Dialectical Reasoning-** Is reasoning which proceeds in the form of a dialogue, with one person making a statement and another making a response to it, which in its turn evokes a further response.

Cognitive Biases- The ability to reason effectively is a key factor in critical thinking, making sound decisions, and solving problems. Unfortunately, several key factors may impair effective reasoning. Cognitive biases are tendencies to think in certain ways. Cognitive biases can lead to systematic deviations from a standard of rationality or good judgment, and are often studied in psychology and behavioral economics.

a) **Affect Heuristic-** Is a mental shortcut that allows people to make decisions and solve problems quickly and efficiently, in which current emotion—fear, pleasure, surprise, etc.—influences decisions. In other words, it is a type of heuristic in which emotional response, or "affect" in psychological terms, plays a lead role. This subconscious process shortens the decision-making process and allows people to function without having to complete an extensive search for information. It is shorter in duration than a mood, occurring rapidly and involuntarily in response to a stimulus.

b) **Availability Heuristic-** In which people base judgments and decisions on how easily information is available in memory. The availability heuristic is a mental shortcut that relies on immediate examples that come to mind. It operates on the notion that if something can be recalled, it must be important. Subsequently, people tend to heavily weigh their judgments toward more recent information, forming new opinions biased toward that latest news.

c) **Hindsight Bias-** Reflects a tendency to overestimate one's s own ability to have predicted or foreseen an event after learning about the outcome.

d) **Fairness Bias-** "Doing the right thing" describes the fairness bias; or that most people are instinctively motivated to do the right thing.

e) **Avoiding Loss Bias-** Refers to people's tendency to strongly prefer avoiding losses to acquiring gains. Some studies suggest that losses are twice as powerful, psychologically, as gains.

f) **Confirmation Bias-** The tendency to look for evidence that will confirm what one believes, rather than looking for evidence that could disconfirm one's beliefs.

g) **Mental Sets-** Falling back on solutions that have worked in the past. In many cases, this is a useful approach that allows us to quickly come up with answers. In some instances, however, this strategy can make it difficult to think of new ways of solving problems. These mental sets can sometimes lead to rigid thinking and can create difficulties in the problem-solving process.

Cognitive Dissonance- In psychology, cognitive dissonance is the mental stress or discomfort experienced by an individual who holds two or more contradictory beliefs, ideas, or values at the same time, or is confronted by new information that conflicts with existing beliefs, ideas, or values. People tend to seek consistency in their beliefs and perceptions. So what happens when one belief conflicts with another previously held belief? The term cognitive dissonance is used to describe the feeling of discomfort that results from holding two conflicting beliefs. When there is a discrepancy between beliefs and behaviors, something must change in order to eliminate or reduce the dissonance.

Intelligence- Is the ability to acquire knowledge, to think and reason effectively, and to deal adaptively with the environment. Intelligence is about problem-solving ability.

History of Measurement- Historically, two scientists with entirely different agendas played seminal roles in the study and measurement of mental skills. The contributions of Sir Francis Galton and Alfred Binet set the stage for later attempts to measure intelligence and discover its causes. Galton's studies of heredity genius and Binet's methods for measuring differences in children's mental skills were important historical milestones in the study of intelligence.

IQ Testing- William Stern developed the intelligence quotient (IQ) which is the ratio of mental age to chronological age, multiplied by 100. Most modern intelligence tests, such as the Wechsler scales, measure an array of mental abilities, including global IQ, and verbal and performance IQs. Other scales provide separate scores for crystallized and fluid intelligence and for analytical, practical, and creative intelligence.

Achievement tests measure what has already been learned, whereas aptitude tests are assumed to measure potential for future learning and performance. Most intelligence tests measure combinations of achievement and aptitude. Three important standards for psychological tests are: reliability (consistency of measurement over time, within tests, and across scorers), validity (successful measurement of the construct and acceptable relations with relevant criterion measures), and standardization (development of norms and standard testing conditions).

IQ scores successfully predict a range of academic, occupational, and life outcomes, including lifespan. Such findings indicate that intelligence tests measure important adaptational skills.

Cultural Influences and Stereotype Threat- Intelligence is determined by interacting heredity and environmental factors. Genes account for between 50 and 70 percent of population variation in IQ. Shared family environment accounts for perhaps one-fourth to one-third of the variance during childhood, but its effects seem to dissipate as people age. Educational experiences also influence mental skills. Heredity establishes a reaction range with upper and lower limits for intellectual potential. Cultural and ethnic differences in intelligence exist but the relative contributions of genetic and environmental factors are still in question.
Beliefs also influence group behavior. Group members can experience stereotype threat if they believe that certain behaviors on their part would confirm a negative stereotype in the minds of others.

Cognitive Approaches- Cognitive process theories explore the specific information-processing and cognitive processes that underlie intellectual ability.

a) **Triarchic Theory of Intelligence -** Addresses both the psychological processes involved in intelligent behavior and the diverse forms that intelligence can take.

b) **Metacognition-** Are the higher-order processes used to plan and regulate task performance. They include problem-solving skills such as identifying problems, formulating hypotheses and strategies, testing them logically, and evaluating performance feedback.

c) **Emotional Intelligence-** Involves the abilities to read others' emotions accurately, to respond to them appropriately, to motivate one, to be aware of one's own emotions, and to regulate and control one's own emotional response.

Animal Intelligence- Animal cognition is the study of the mental capacities of animals. It has developed out of comparative psychology, including the study of animal conditioning and learning; but has also been strongly influenced by research in ethology, behavioral ecology, and evolutionary psychology. Beginning around 1960, a "cognitive revolution" in research on humans gradually spurred a similar transformation of research with animals. Inference to processes not directly observable became acceptable and then commonplace. An important proponent of this shift in thinking was Donald O. Hebb, who argued that "mind" is simply a name for processes in the head that control complex behavior, and that it is both necessary and possible to infer those processes from behavior. Animals came to be seen as "goal seeking agents that acquire, store, retrieve, and internally process information at many levels of cognitive complexity."

Creativity- Is the ability to produce something that is both new and valuable. One component of creativity is the ability to break away from conventional approaches when the occasion demands it and to engage in divergent thinking. Divergent thinking is the generation of novel ideas that depart from the norm. In part, this means being able to apply concepts or propositions from one domain to another unrelated domain in a manner that produces a new insight. It also means refusing to be constrained by traditional approaches to a problem.

Unit Seven Practice Quiz

1. Which bias states that "doing the right thing" is what most people are motivated to do?
   A) Availability bias
   B) Confirmation bias
   C) Fairness bias
   D) Hindsight bias

2. True or False: Deductive reasoning occurs from the bottom up; creating a general principle from general facts.
   A) True
   B) False

3. Chantal believes that all small dogs are kind. She witnesses a small dog attack her neighbor and feels confused because her beliefs conflicted with what she saw. This is known as:
   A) Cognitive dissonance
   B) Neural conflict
   C) Cultural control
   D) Availability heuristic

4. True or False: Formulating a hypothesis is a type of metacognition.
   A) True
   B) False

5. Which heuristic involves forming smaller steps in order to reach a bigger goal?
   A) Approach
   B) Availability
   C) Means-end
   D) Subgoal

6. Which of the following could be an example emotional intelligence?
   A) Sympathizing with yourself
   B) Empathizing with another person
   C) Hearing your own thoughts consciously
   D) Being able to predict somebody's future

7. Which part of the mind includes your awareness at the present moment?
   A) Conscious
   B) Subconscious

8. Which kind of reasoning proceeds in the form of a back-and-forth conversation?
   A) Subconscious
   B) Inductive
   C) Dialectical
   D) Deductive

Answer Key: 1=C, 2=B, 3=A, 4=A, 5=D, 6=B, 7=A, 8=C

Unit Eight: Human Development

Learning Objectives
After completing this unit, you should be able to:

1. Discuss Piaget's stages of cognitive development
2. Discuss Erikson's eight stages of development
3. Discuss how infants and children develop physically, socially, emotionally, and cognitively
4. Discuss major developmental changes that occur in the prenatal stage
5. Discuss major development changes that occur in the infancy stage
6. Discuss major developmental changes that occur in adolescents and adulthood

Development over the Lifespan- Developmental psychology examines biological, physical, psychological, and behavioral changes that occur as we age. Questions about the influence of nature and nurture, critical and sensitive periods, continuity versus discontinuity, and stability versus change have guided much developmental research. Cross-sectional designs compare different age groups at one point in time. A longitudinal design repeatedly tests the same age group as it grows older. Sequential designs test several groups at one point in time and then again as they grow older.

Theoretical Perspectives- Theories of development usually deal with changes over time in a particular area of psychological functioning; thus there are theories of social development, moral development, and personality development.

Piaget's Stages of Cognitive Development- Piaget's theory of cognitive development describes how children's thinking (their ability to solve problems) changes as they get older.

a) **Sensorimotor Stage-** From birth to around the age of two, infants in the sensorimotor stage understand their world primarily through sensory experiences and physical (motor) interactions with objects. Children during this age now grasp the concept of object permanence, the understanding that an object continues to exist even when it no longer can be seen. At this stage they start to exhibit the emergence of symbolic thought.

b) **Preoperational Stage-** At about the age of two, children enter the preoperational stage, in which they can represent the world symbolically through words and mental images but do not yet understand basic mental operations or rules. Symbolic thinking enables the child to engage in pretend play. Thinking displays egocentrism (difficulty in viewing the world from someone else's perspective), irreversibility, and concentration. The child at this stage does not understand conversation, the principle that the basic properties of objects, such as their volume, mass, or quantity, stay the same even though their outward appearance may change.

c) **Concrete Operational Stage-** From about the ages seven to twelve, children in the concrete operational stage can perform basic mental operations concerning problems that involve tangible objects and situations. The child can think logically about concrete events and grasp concepts of conversation and serial ordering.

d) **Formal Operational Stage-** Piaget's model ends with the formal operational stage, in which individuals can think logically about concrete and abstract problems, form hypotheses, and systematically test them.

Current Views of Cognitive Development- Cognitive development is a field of study in neuroscience and psychology focusing on a child's development, in terms of information processing, conceptual resources, perceptual skill, language learning, and other aspects of brain development and cognitive psychology, compared to an adult's point of view. A large portion of research has gone into understanding how a child imagines the world. Jean Piaget was a major force in the establishment of this field, forming his "theory of cognitive development". In recent years, however, alternative models have been advanced, including information-processing theory, neo-Piagetian theories of cognitive development, which aim to integrate Piaget's ideas with more recent models and concepts in developmental and cognitive science, theoretical cognitive neuroscience, and social-constructivist approaches.

A major controversy in cognitive development has been "nature and nurture", that is, the question of whether cognitive development is mainly determined by an individual's innate qualities (nature), or by their personal experiences (nurture). However, it is now recognized by most experts that this is a false dichotomy: there is overwhelming evidence from biological and behavioral sciences that, from the earliest points in development, gene activity interacts with events and experiences in the environment.

Vygotsky's Theory of Sociocultural Influences- Sociocultural theory is emerging theory in psychology that looks at the important contributions that society makes to individual development. This theory stresses the interaction between developing people and the culture in which they live. Sociocultural theory grew from the work of seminal psychologist Lev Vygotsky, who believed that parents, caregivers, peers and the culture at large were responsible for the development of higher order functions. According to Vygotsky, "Every function in the child's cultural development appears twice: first, on the social level, and later, on the individual level; first, between people (interpsychological) and then inside the child (intrapsychological). This applies equally to voluntary attention, to logical memory, and to the formation of concepts. All the higher functions originate as actual relationships between individuals."

Sociocultural theory focuses, not only on how adults and peers influence individual learning, but also on how cultural beliefs and attitudes impact how instruction and learning take place. An important concept in sociocultural theory is known as the zone of proximal development. According to Vygotsky, the zone of proximal development "is the distance between the actual development level as determined by independent problem solving and the level of potential development as determined through problem solving under adult guidance or in collaboration with more capable peers." Essentially, it includes all of the knowledge and skills that a person cannot yet understand or perform on their own, but is capable of learning with guidance. Vygotksy's theory is guided by six major assumptions:

1. Children develop through informal and formal conversations with adults.
2. The first few years of life are critical for development, as this is where thought and language become increasingly independent.
3. Complex mental activities begin as basic social activities.
4. Children can perform more difficult tasks with the help of a more advanced individual.
5. Tasks that are challenging promote cognitive development growth.
6. Play is important and allows children to stretch themselves cognitively.

Erikson's Stages of Development- Psychologist Erik Erikson believed that personality develops through confronting a series of eight psychosocial stages, each involving a different crisis over how we view ourselves in relation to other people and the world. Each crisis is present throughout life but takes on special importance during a particular age period. Four of these crises occur in infancy and childhood.

a) **Basic Trust versus Basic Mistrust-** This stage occurs in infancy during the first year. Depending on how well our needs are met and how much love we receive during the first year of life, we develop a basic trust or mistrust of the world.

b) **Autonomy versus Shame and Doubt-** This stage occurs in toddlerhood ages 1-2, when children begin to exercise their individuality. If parents unduly restrict children or make harsh toileting training demands, children develop shame and doubt about their abilities and later lack the courage to be independent.

c) **Initiative versus Guilt-** From age 3 through age 5, also known as early childhood, children display great curiosity about the world. If they are allowed freedom to explore, they develop a sense of initiative. If they are held back or punished, they develop guilt about their desires and suppress their curiosity.

d) **Industry versus Inferiority-** From age 6 until puberty which is typically around age 12, also known as middle childhood, the child's life expands into school and peer activities, Children who experience pride and encouragement in mastering tasks develop industry – a striving to achieve. Repeated failure and lack of praise for trying leads to a sense of inferiority.

e) **Identity versus Role Confusion-** During adolescence, ages 12-19, children explore their independence and develop a sense of self. Those who receive proper encouragement and reinforcement through personal exploration will emerge from this stage with a strong sense of self and a feeling of independence and control. Those who remain unsure of their beliefs and desires will feel insecure and confused about themselves and the future. Completing this stage successfully leads to fidelity, which Erikson described as an ability to live by society's standards and expectations.

f) **Intimacy versus Isolation-** This stage covers the period of early adulthood, ages 20-39, when people are exploring personal relationships. Erikson believed it was vital that people developed close, committed relationships with other people. Those who are successful at this step will form relationships that are committed and secure. Remember that each step builds on skills learned in previous steps. Erikson believed that a strong sense of personal identity was important for developing intimate relationships. Studies have demonstrated that those with a poor sense of self tend to have less committed relationships and are more likely to suffer emotional isolation, loneliness, and depression. Successful resolution of this stage results in the virtue known as love. It is marked by the ability to form lasting, meaningful relationships with other people.

g) **Generativity versus Stagnation-** During adulthood, ages 40-64, also known as middle adulthood, we continue to build our lives, focusing on our career and family. Those who are successful during this phase will feel that they are contributing to the world by being active in their home and community. Those who fail to attain this skill will feel unproductive and uninvolved in the world. Care is the virtue achieved when this stage is handled successfully. Being proud of one's accomplishments, watching one's children grow into adults, and developing a sense of unity with a life partner are important accomplishments of this stage.

h) **Integrity versus Despair-** This phase occurs during old age, ages 65 and over, considered late adulthood, and is focused on reflecting back on life. Those who are unsuccessful during this stage will feel that their life has been wasted and will experience many regrets. The individual will be left with feelings of bitterness and despair. Those who feel proud of their accomplishments will feel a sense of integrity. Successfully completing this phase means looking back with few regrets and a general feeling of satisfaction. These individuals will attain wisdom, even when confronting death.

Kohlberg's Theory of Moral Development- Proposed moral reasoning proceeds through three main levels of moral reasoning. The development of moral behavior is linked to children's cognitive, emotional, and social development.

a) **Preconventional Moral Reasoning-** Based on anticipated punishments or rewards.

b) **Conventional Moral Reasoning-** Based on conformity to social expectations, laws, and duties.

c) **Postconventional Moral Reasoning-** Based on well-thought-out, general moral principles.

Early Development

Prenatal- Our genetic blueprint sets forth a path of prenatal development that consists of three stages. The **germinal stage** comprises approximately the first two weeks of development, beginning when a sperm fertilizes a female egg (ovum). The fertilized egg is called a **zygote** and through repeated cell division it becomes a mass of cells that attaches to the mother's uterus at about 10-14 days after conception. The **embryonic stage** is next, the cell mass, now called an embryo, develops from the end of week two through week eight after conception. Two life-support structures, the placenta and umbilical cord develop at this stage. The **fetus** develops from week nine after conception until birth. Muscles strengthen and other bodily systems develop.

Infancy- Newborns distinguish between different visual patterns, sounds, odors, and tastes. They display perceptual preferences and learn through classical and operant conditioning. Biology and environment jointly steer children's physical and psychological development.

Attachment- In humans, attachment refers to the strong emotional bond that develops between children and their primary caregivers. Infant caregiver attachment develops in phases. Infants experience periods of stranger anxiety (distress over contact with unfamiliar people) which often emerges at around 6-7 months, and separation anxiety (distress over separation from a primary caregiver) which often appears at around 12-16 months. The attachment process in infancy develops in three phases: **Indiscriminate attachment behavior-** newborns cry, vocalize, and smile toward everyone, and these behaviors evoke caregiving from adults. **Discriminate attachment behavior-** around three months of age, infants direct their attachment behaviors more toward familiar caregivers than toward strangers. **Specific attachment behavior-** By seven or eight months of age, infants develop a meaningful attachment to specific caregivers. The caregiver becomes a secure base from which the infant can explore the environment. Secure attachment is associated with better developmental outcomes than is insecure attachment.

Cognitive Development: Language- Human language is symbolic and structured, conveys meaning, is generative, and permits displacement. Language facilitates cooperative social systems and knowledge transmission. A language's surface structure refers to how symbols are combined; the deep structure refers to the underlying meaning of symbols. Language elements are hierarchically arranged: from phonemes (the smallest unit of speech sound in language that can signal a difference in meaning) to morphemes (the smallest units of meaning in language), words, phrases, and sentences. Scientists believe that humans have evolved an innate capacity for acquiring language. Infants can perceive all the phonemes that exist in all the languages of the world. Between 6 and 12 months of age, their speech discrimination narrows to include only the sounds specific to their native tongue. By ages 4-5, most children have learned basic grammatical rules from combining words into meaningful sentences.

Language development depends on innate brain mechanisms that permit the learning and production of language; provided the child is exposed to an appropriate linguistic environment during a sensitive period that extends from early childhood to puberty. Language influences what people think and how effectively they think. Expansion of vocabulary allows people to encode and process information in more sophisticated ways.

Influences of Gender Development

   a) **Biological-** The 23rd chromosome in a mother's egg cell is always an X chromosome. If the 23rd chromosome in the father's sperm cell is an X, the child will be genetically female (XX); if it is a Y, the child will be genetically male (XY). Teratogens such as maternal illnesses, environmental toxins, and drugs can cause abnormal prenatal development.

   b) **Cognitive-** The theory proposes the interaction of mental schema and social experience in directing gender role behavior. The cognitive approach focuses upon the child's "understanding". A child's understanding refers to the way he/she perceives and tackles a phenomenon. Information about gender is organized into sets of beliefs about the sexes i.e. gender schema (plural schemata or schemas) is a mental framework that organizes and guides a child's understanding of information relevant to gender. Example: information about which toys are for girls and which toys are for boys forms schema that guides behavior.

   c) **Learning-** Studies have shown that children's upbringing and social environments also impact their developing gender identities. Children's interests, preferences, behaviors and overall self-concept are strongly influenced by parental and authority figure teachings regarding sexual stereotypes, occurring in or before the early portion of middle childhood. Children who are taught that certain traits or activities are appropriate or inappropriate for them, because they are a girl or a boy, do tend to internalize and be influenced by these teachings in later life. For instance, girls who are informed that boys are innately better at math than they are, may report that they dislike math and disclaim their interest in that subject. They may go on to believe that they are not good at this academic subject, and to perform poorly on math tests and homework assignments.

   Children learn vicariously, in part, through their observation and imitation of what they see their primary caregivers doing. They tend to imitate and internalize what they see and then repeat those patterns in their own lives as though they had come up with them independently. Children raised watching their parents adhere to strict gender-stereotyped roles are, in general, more likely to take on those roles themselves as adults, than are peers whose parents provided less stereotyped, more androgynous models for behavior.

Adolescents- Adolescence is a socially constructed transition period between childhood and adulthood. In contrast, puberty is a biologically based period of rapid maturation. Physical and perceptual functioning typically peak in young adulthood. Adolescents may show egocentric social thinking. Their abstract thinking blossoms, and information-processing abilities improve.

Beginning in early adulthood, information processing speed slows, but many intellectual abilities do not begin to decline reliably until late adulthood. The search for identity is a key task of adolescence. During adolescence, peer relationships become important. Most teens maintain good relationships with their parents. Overall, for most teens, daily emotional experience becomes less positive as they move into and through early adolescence.

Adulthood- In many traditional cultures, marriage is the key transitional event into adulthood. Through socialization, males develop skills that will enable them to provide for a family of their own, and females learn skills needed to care for children and run a household. Marriage signifies that each partner has acquired these skills and is capable of raising a family. For many couples, marital satisfaction tends to decline in the years following the birth of children but increases later in adulthood.

Old Age- Retirement is an important milestone. Some adults view it as a reminder that they are growing older, but look forward to leisure, and other opportunities they were unable to pursue during their careers. The decision to retire or keep working typically involves many factors, such as one's feelings about one's job, leisure activities, physical health, and family relationships. Part of being human is the fact that we are mortal. Understandably, the elderly are more accepting of their own mortality than any other age group. Many terminally ill patients experience similar psychological reactions, as they cope with impending death, but beliefs and feelings about death vary with culture and age, and there is no normal way to approach death.

Unit Eight Practice Quiz

1. Which of the following is not one of Vygotsky's theoretical assumptions?
   A) Children develop through informal and formal conversations with adults
   B) Complex mental activities began as basic social activities
   C) Children must overcome crises in order to develop efficiently
   D) Play is important and allows children to stretch themselves cognitively

2. True or False: The preoperational stage includes symbolic thinking and egocentrism.
   A) True
   B) False

3. Which of the following is the last stage of Erikson's theory of development?
   A) Autonomy vs. shame and doubt
   B) Integrity vs. despair
   C) Identity vs. role confusion
   D) Industry vs. inferiority

4. What chromosome defines the baby's gender?
   A) 21st
   B) 23rd

5. All the following are stages of Piaget's theory of cognitive development EXCEPT:
   A) Sensorimotor
   B) Preoperational
   C) Operational
   D) Postoperational

6. Which of the following is an example of separation anxiety?
   A) Crying when mother leaves the room
   B) Playing with strangers
   C) Sleeping
   D) Overeating

7. True or False: Children are born with specific attachment behavior.
   A) True
   B) False

8. How many stages are there in Kohlberg's theory of moral development?
   A) Five
   B) Two
   C) Eight
   D) Three

Answer Key: 1=C, 2=A, 3=B, 4=B, 5=D, 6=A, 7=B, 8=D

Unit Nine: Personality

Learning Objectives
After completing this unit, you should be able to:

1. Discuss how unconscious factors determine our behavior
2. Discuss how psychological defenses determine our behavior
3. Discuss how childhood factors influence adult personality
4. Describe the structure of personality
5. Discuss how evolution influences personality development
6. Discuss how biological factors influence personality development
7. Discuss how social-cognitive theories account for the inconsistencies of behavior across situations
8. Discuss how cultural influences and gender roles account for differences in personality development
9. Discuss how modern perspectives and trait theories approach are used to assess personality

Theories of Personality
The concept of personality arises from the fascinating spectrum of human individuality. We observe that people differ meaningfully in the ways they customarily think, feel, and act. These distinctive behavior patterns help define one's identity as a person. The concept of personality also rests on the observation that a given person seems to behave somewhat consistently over time and across different situations. From this perceived consistency comes the notion of personality traits that characterize and individual's customary ways of responding to his or her world. Combining these notions of individuality and consistency, we can define personality as the distinctive and relatively enduring ways of thinking, feeling, and acting that characterize a person's responses to life's situations.

Scientifically useful personality theories organize existing knowledge, allow the prediction of future events, and stimulate the discovery of new knowledge.

Psychodynamic Approaches- The first formal theory of personality was advanced by Sigmund Freud. Psychodynamic theorists look for the causes of behavior in a dynamic interplay of inner forces that often conflict with one another. Freud's theory of psychoanalysis describes people as having two fundamental needs or motives: sex and aggression. Unbridled sex and aggression are not generally accepted among the general population, so there are social pressures on children to restrain themselves from acting on these needs. A child's personality develops as it figures out how to get basic needs met while still making mom and dad happy.

Freud divided personality into three separate but interacting structures: id, ego, and superego.

  a) **Id-** Is the innermost core of the personality, the only structure present at birth, and the source of all psychic energy. It exists totally within the unconscious mind. The id has no direct contact with reality and functions in a totally irrational manner. Operating according to the pleasure principle, it seeks immediate gratification or release, regardless of rational considerations and environmental realities.

  b) **Ego-** Has direct contact with reality and functions primarily at a conscious level. It operates according to the reality principle, testing reality to decide when and under what conditions the id can safely discharge its impulses and satisfy its needs.

  c) **Superego-** The moral arm of the personality. Developing by age four or five, the superego contains the traditional values and ideals of family and society.

Defense Mechanisms- Unconscious mental operations that deny or distort reality. Some of the defense mechanisms permit the release of impulses from the id in disguised forms that will not conflict with forces in the external world or with the prohibitions of the superego.

  a) **Repression-** An active defense process pushes anxiety-arousing impulses or memories into the unconscious mind.

  b) **Denial-** A person refuses to acknowledge anxiety-arousing aspects of the environment. The denial may involve either the emotions connected with the event or the event itself.

  c) **Displacement-** An unacceptable or dangerous impulse is regressed, then directed at a safer substitute target.

  d) **Intellectualization-** The emotion connected with an upsetting event is repressed, and the situation is dealt with as an intellectually interesting event.

  e) **Projection-** An unacceptable impulse is regressed, then attributed to (projected onto) other people.

  f) **Rationalization-** A person constructs a false but plausible explanation or excuse for an anxiety-arousing behavior or event that has already occurred.

  g) **Reaction Formation-** An anxiety-arousing impulse is repressed, and its psychic energy finds release in an exaggerated expression of the opposite behavior.

  h) **Sublimation-** A repressed impulse is released in the form of a socially acceptable or even admired behavior.

Psychosexual Stages- Freud proposed that children pass through a series of psychosexual stages during which the id's pleasure-seeking tendencies are focused on specific pleasure-sensitive areas of the body. Potential deprivations or overindulgence can arise during any of these stages, resulting in fixation, a state of arrested psychosexual development in which instincts are focused on a particular psychic theme. Regression is a psychological retreat to an earlier psychosexual stage.

   a) **Oral Stage-** The first stage is the oral stage, which occurs during infancy. Infants gain primary satisfaction from taking in food and from sucking on a breast, thumb, or some other object. Freud proposed that either excessive gratification or frustration of oral needs can result in fixation on oral themes of self-indulgence or dependency as an adult.

   b) **Anal Stage-** In the second and third years of life, children enter the anal stage, and pleasure becomes focused on the process of elimination. According to Freud, harsh toilet training can produce compulsions, overemphasis on cleanliness, obsessive concerns with orderliness, and insistence on rigid rules and rituals.

   c) **Phallic Stage-** The most controversial of Freud's stages is the phallic stage, which begins at 4 to 5 years of age. This is the time when children begin to derive pleasure from their sexual organs. Freud believed that during this stage of early sexual awakenings, the male child experiences erotic feelings toward his mother and views the father as a rival. This conflictual situation involving love for the mother and hostility toward the father is called the **Oedipus complex**. Girls, meanwhile, discover that they lack a penis, blame the mother for their lack of what Freud considered the more desirable sex organ, and wish to bear their father's child as a substitute for the penis they lack. The female counterpart of the Oedipus complex was termed the **Electra complex**. Freud believed that the phallic stage is a major milestone in the development of gender identity.

   d) **Latency Stage-** As the phallic stage draws to a close at about 6 years of age, children enter the latency stage, during which sexuality becomes dormant for about six years.

   e) **Genital Stage-** Sexuality normally reemerges in adolescence as the beginning of a lifelong genital stage, in which erotic impulses find direct expression in sexual relationships.

Jungian Theory- Analytical Psychology is Jung's term for his theory and practice of psychology. He coined the term to distinguish it from Freud's form of psychotherapy, which Freud called psychoanalysis. The phrase most commonly used today to describe Jung's model of therapeutic practice is Jungian analysis. Whichever term is used, for Jung, psychoanalysis is ideally an attempt to bring conscious and unconscious elements of the psyche into balance. Jung expanded Freud's notion of the unconscious in unique directions. He believed that humans possess not only a **personal unconscious** based on their life experiences, but also a

collective unconscious that consists of memories accumulated throughout the entire history of the human race. These memories are represented by **archetypes**, inherited tendencies to interpret experiences in certain ways.

Object Relations- Focuses on the images or mental representations that people form of themselves and other people, as a result of early experiences with caregivers. Whether realistic or distorted, these internal representations of important adults become the lenses, or working models, through which later social interactions are viewed, and these relational themes exert an unconscious influence on a person's relationships throughout life.

Humanistic Approaches- Humanistic theories emphasize the subjective experiences of the individual and thus deal with the perceptual and cognitive processes.

a) **George Kelly's Personal Construct Theory-** Addresses the manner in which people differ in their constructions of reality by their **personal constructs**, cognitive categories into which they sort the people and events in their lives and which they use to categorize their experiences.

b) **Carl Roger's Theory of Self-** Attaches central importance to the role of the self and an innate drive toward self-actualization. Experiences that are incongruous with the established self-concept produce threat and may result in denial or distortion of reality. Conditional positive regard may result in unrealistic conditions of worth that conflict with **self-actualization,** the highest realization of human potential. Roger's theory helped stimulate a great deal of research on the self-concept, including studies on the origins of **self-esteem**, how positively or negatively we feel about ourselves; **self-enhancement**, a strong and pervasive tendency to gain and preserve a positive self-image; **and self- verification**, the need to confirm the self-concept, and self-concept change.

Genetic Approaches- Genetic factors account for as much as half of the group variance in personality test scores, with individual experiences accounting for most of the remainder. Evolutionary theories of personality attribute some personality dispositions to genetically controlled mechanisms based on natural selection.

a) **Eysenck's Extraversion-Stability Model-** Psychologist Hans Eysenck maintained that normal personality can be understood in terms of only two basic dimensions. These dimensions of Introversion-Extraversion and Stability-Instability (sometimes as in the Big Five, called Neuroticism) blend together to form all of the more specific traits. In Eysenck's theory, Introversion-Extraversion reflects a person's customary level of arousal, whereas Stability-Instability represents the suddenness with which shifts in arousal occur.

b) **Temperament-** Refers to the individual differences in emotional and behavioral studies that appear so early in life that they are assumed to have a biological basis. Temperament is stable during childhood and into adulthood. Inhibited children and adults appear to have highly reactive amygdalas that trigger fear responses to unfamiliar people and situations.

Environmental Influences- Personality is a product of interacting biological and environmental influences. Children inherit different biologies which influence how their environment, including culture, affects them.

Social Learning- Gender role socialization provides us with gender schemas, organized mental structures that contain our understanding of the attributes and behaviors that are appropriate and expected for males and females. Within a given culture, gender schemas tell us what the typical man or woman should be like.

a) Social learning theory posits that learning is a cognitive process that takes place in a social context, and can occur purely through observation or direct instruction, even in the absence of motor reproduction or direct reinforcement. In addition to the observation of behavior, learning also occurs through the observation of rewards and punishments, a process known as vicarious reinforcement. The theory expands on traditional behavioral theories, in which behavior is governed solely by reinforcements, by placing emphasis on the important roles of various internal processes in the learning individual.

b) Social learning theory integrates behavioral and cognitive theories of learning, in order to provide a comprehensive model to account for the wide range of learning experiences that occur in the real world. Key tenets of social learning theory are: Learning is not purely behavioral, rather, it is a cognitive process that takes place in a social context; learning can occur by observing a behavior and by observing the consequences of the behavior (vicarious reinforcement); learning involves observation, extraction of information from those observations, and making decisions about the performance of the behavior (observational learning or modeling). Thus, learning can occur without an observable change in behavior; reinforcement plays a role in learning but is not entirely responsible for learning; the learner is not a passive recipient of information. Cognition, environment, and behavior all mutually influence each other (reciprocal determinism).

c) Social learning theory draws heavily on the concept of modeling, or learning by observing a behavior. Bandura outlined three types of modeling stimuli: **Live model** in which an actual person is demonstrating the desired behavior; **Verbal instruction** in which an individual describes the desired behavior in detail and instructs the participant in how to engage in the behavior; and **Symbolic** in which modeling occurs by means of the media, including movies, television, Internet, literature, and radio. Stimuli can be either real or fictional characters.

d) Exactly what information is gleaned from observation is influenced by the type of model, as well as by a series of cognitive and behavioral processes. **Attention-** in order to learn, observers must attend to the modeled behavior. Attention is impacted by the characteristics of the observer (e.g., perceptual abilities, cognitive abilities, arousal, past performance) and characteristics of the behavior or event (e.g., relevance, novelty, affective valence, and functional value). **Retention-** in order to reproduce an observed behavior, observers must be able to remember features of the behavior. Again, this process is influenced by observer characteristics (cognitive capabilities, cognitive rehearsal) and event characteristics (complexity). **Reproduction-** to reproduce a behavior, the observer must organize responses in accordance with the model. Observer characteristics affecting reproduction include physical and cognitive capabilities and previous performance. **Motivation-** the decision to reproduce (or refrain from reproducing) an observed behavior is dependent on the motivations and expectations of the observer, including anticipated consequences and internal standards.

e) An important factor in social learning theory is the concept of **reciprocal determinism**. This notion states that just as an individual's behavior is influenced by the environment, the environment is also influenced by the individual's behavior. In other words, a person's behavior, environment, and personal qualities all reciprocally influence each other.

Cultural Influences- Cultures differ along several important dimensions, including complexity, tightness, and individualism-collectivism, all of which can effect personality development. People from individualistic cultures tend to describe themselves in terms of personal traits, abilities, or dispositions, whereas those from collectivistic cultures are more likely to describe themselves in social identity terms.

Modern Perspectives/Trait Approach- The goals of trait theorists are to describe the basic classes of behavior that define personality, to devise ways of measuring individual differences in personality traits, and to use these measures to understand and predict a person's behavior. Personality traits are relatively stable cognitive, emotional, and behavioral characteristics of people that help establish their individual identities and distinguish them from others.

a) **Factor Analysis-** Is used to identify clusters of behaviors that are highly correlated (positively or negatively) with one another, but not with behaviors in other clusters. Such behavior clusters can be viewed as reflecting a basic dimension, or trait, on which people vary. These behavioral patterns define a general factor, or dimension that we might label introversion-extraversion.

b) **The Big Five-** The Big Five personality traits represent an attempt to identify traits for which scores correlate highly with each other, because they are fundamental to describing what personality is all about. Proponents of the Big Five believe that, when a person is placed at a specific point on each of these five dimensions by means of a psychological test, behavior ratings, or direct observations of behavior, the essence of his or her personality is captured. The Big Five factors are: **Openness-** inquiring, independent and curious behavior; **Conscientiousness-** dependable and self-controlled behavior; **Extraversion-** outgoing and socially adaptable behavior; **Agreeableness-** conforming, likable, and trusting behavior; and **Neuroticism-** anxiety and excitable behavior.

Unit Nine Practice Quiz

1. Which of the following is NOT that the part of Eysenck's Extraversion-Stability "Big Five" model?
   A) Introversion
   B) Neuroticism
   C) Openness
   D) Confidence

2. True or False: A person who has high introversion is very social and outgoing.
   A) True
   B) False

3. Which part of Carl Rogers' theory of self includes the highest realization of human potential?
   A) Self-actualization
   B) Self-esteem
   C) Self-verification
   D) Self-verification

4. True or False: According to Bandura, a "live model" of learning involves demonstrating a behavior.
   A) True
   B) False

5. The theory that encompasses the idea that behavior is influenced by the environment and vice versa is known as:
   A) Self-actualization
   B) Extraversion
   C) Reciprocal determinism
   D) Cognitive dissonance

6. Which of the following is NOT a crucial element of learning?
   A) Retention
   B) Closure
   C) Motivation
   D) Reproduction

7. True or False: The collective unconscious is limited to one's own life experiences.
   A) True
   B) False

8. Which stage of Freud's theory of psychosexual development includes the Oedipus and Electra complexes?
A) Oral
B) Phallic
C) Genital
D) Latent

Answer Key: 1=D, 2=B, 3=A, 4=A, 5=C, 6=B, 7=B, 8=B

Unit Ten: Psychological Disorders and Therapies

Learning Objectives
After completing this unit, you should be able to:

1. Discuss the scope and nature of psychological disorders
2. Discuss the different types of anxiety and how it is manifested in psychological disorders
3. Discuss the biological, psychological, and environmental causal factors common in mood disorders
4. Discuss the features and causes of schizophrenia
5. Discuss the principles of therapy applied to families and groups
6. Discuss the different therapy approaches utilized in psychotherapy
7. Discuss how biological approaches, including drugs and psychosurgery, are applied to the treatment of behavior disorders

The branch of psychology that deals with psychological disorders is called abnormal psychology. The classic way to define abnormality, or disorder, is in terms of patterns of thoughts, feelings, or behaviors that interfere with a person's ability to function at work, in relationships, or at leisure activities.

Stress- The term stress appears regularly in our everyday discourse. Psychologists have conceived of stress in three different ways: as a stimulus, as a response, and as an ongoing interaction between and organism and its environment. Some scientists define stress as events that place strong demands on us. These demanding or threatening situations are stressors.

   a) **Physiology-** Sensory feedback from our body's response can cause us to reappraise how stressful a situation is and if our resources are sufficient to cope with it. Endocrinologist Han Selye described a physiological response pattern to strong and prolonged stressors. The general adaption syndrome (GAS) consists of three phases: alarm, resistance, and exhaustion. In response to a physical or psychological stressor, organisms exhibit an immediate increase in physiological arousal, as the body mobilizes itself to respond to the threat. This **alarm** reaction occurs because of the sudden activation of the sympathetic nervous system and the release of stress hormones by the endocrine system. During **resistance**, the body's resources are mobilized by the continued outpouring of stress hormones by the endocrine system, particularly the adrenal glands. If the stressor is intense and persists too long, the body will eventually reach a stage of **exhaustion**, in which there is increased vulnerability to disease and, in some extreme cases, collapse and even death.

   b) **Optimism and Pessimism-** Our beliefs about how things are likely to turn out also play an important role in dealing with stressors. Recent research indicates that optimistic people are at a lower risk for anxiety and depression when they confront stressful events. Optimistic people tend to interpret their troubles as temporary, controllable, and specific to one situation, whereas pessimists view their problems as uncontrollable, long-lasting, and generalized across life domains.

c) **Control-** The fact that people differ so dramatically in their responses to stressful events has prompted many health psychologists to search for personal and environmental factors that make people less reactive to stressful events. So called protective factors are environmental or personal resources that create resilience, helping people to cope more effectively with stressful events. Vulnerability and protective factors make people more or less susceptible to stressors. Social support is an important protective factor, having both direct and buffering effects that help people cope with stress. Recent attention has focused on two classes of cognitive strategies, known as dissociation and association. A **dissociative** strategy involves dissociating, or distracting, oneself from the painful sensory input. **Associative** strategies involve focusing attention on the physical sensations and studying them in a detached and unemotional fashion, taking care not to label them as painful or difficult to tolerate.

d) **Coping Methods-** Although people may respond to a stressor in many ways, coping strategies can be divided into three broad classes. **Problem-focused** coping strategies attempt to confront and directly deal with the demands of the situation or to change the situation so that it is no longer stressful. Rather than dealing directly with the stressful situation, **emotion-focused** coping strategies attempt to manage the emotional responses that result from it. A third class of coping strategies involves **seeking social support**, that is, turning to others for assistance and emotional support in times of stress. Problem-focused coping and seeking social support generally relate to better adjustment than emotion-focused coping. However, in situations involving low personal control, emotion-focused coping may be the most appropriate and effective strategy.

Abnormal Behavior- Abnormal behavior is defined as behavior that is personally distressing, personally dysfunctional, and/or so culturally deviant that other people judge it to be inappropriate or maladaptive. Behavior that is judged to reflect a psychological disorder typically is: distressing to the person or to other people; dysfunctional, maladaptive, or self-defeating; and/or socially deviant in a way that arouses discomfort in others and cannot be attributed to environmental causes.

There is a great variety in the behaviors that are judged to be abnormal in contemporary society. Indeed, no less than 374 disorders are included in the current manual of the American Psychiatric Association- the DSM-IV-TR (Diagnostic and Statistical Manual of Mental Disorders, Fourth Edition Textual Revision).

a) **DSM-IV-TR-** The Diagnostic and Statistical Manual of Mental Disorders, Fourth Edition Textual Revision, is the most widely used diagnostic classification system in the United States. For each of its more than 350 diagnostic categories, the manual contains detailed lists of observable behaviors that must be present in order for a diagnosis to be made. Reflecting an awareness of interacting personal and environmental factors, the DSM allows diagnostic information to be represented along five dimensions, or axes, that take both the person and her or his life situation into account. The DSM-IV-TR is a categorical classification system. **Axis I** represents current clinical symptoms, that is, the deviant behaviors or thought processes that are occurring at the present time. **Axis II** reflects long-standing personality disorders or mental retardation, both of which can influence the person's behavior and response to treatment. **Axis III** notes any medical conditions that might be relevant. Reflecting the vulnerability stress model, the clinician rates the intensity of psychosocial or environmental problems in the person's recent life on **Axis IV**, and the person's coping resources, as reflected in recent adaptive functioning on **Axis V**.

b) **Projective Testing-** Presents subjects with ambiguous stimuli and ask for interpretation of them. It is assumed that interpretations of such stimuli give clues to important internal processes. **The Rorschach Test** consists of 10 inkblots; the person being tested is shown each one in succession and asked what each looks like. Many find this test useful for gaining insight into unconscious processes, and the test seems to be especially valuable for detecting psychotic thought disorders. **The Thematic Apperception Test** (TAT) consists of a series of pictures derived from paintings, drawings, and magazine illustrations. The TAT typically relies on the subjective interpretation of tests responses, which can result in different interpretations of the same stories.

c) **Objective Tests-** Psychological testing refers to the administration of psychological tests. A psychological test is "an objective and standardized measure of a sample of behavior". The term 'sample of behavior' refers to an individual's performance on tasks that have usually been prescribed beforehand. Psychological tests are typically, but not necessarily, a series of tasks to be performed or problems to be solved. The questions that make up a paper-and-pencil test, the most common type of test, usually involve a series of items. Performance on these questions produces a test score. A score on a well-constructed test is believed to reflect a psychological construct, such as achievement in a school subject, cognitive ability, aptitude, emotional functioning, personality, etc. Differences in test scores are thought to reflect individual differences in the construct the test is supposed to measure. The technical term for the science behind psychological testing is psychometrics. A psychological test is an instrument designed to measure unobserved constructs, also known as latent variables. Psychological tests can strongly resemble questionnaires, which are also designed to measure unobserved constructs, but differ, in that psychological tests ask for a respondent's maximum performance, whereas a questionnaire asks for the respondent's typical performance. A useful psychological test must be both valid (there is evidence to support the specified interpretation of the test results) and reliable (internally consistent or give consistent results over time, across raters, etc.).

Objective tests have a restricted response format, such as allowing for true or false answers or rating using an ordinal scale. Prominent examples of objective personality tests include the Minnesota Multiphasic Personality Inventory, Millon Clinical Multiaxial Inventory-III, Child Behavior Checklist, Symptom Checklist 90 and the Beck Depression Inventory.

Objective personality tests can be designed for use in business for potential employees, such as the NEO-PI, the 16PF, and the OPQ (Occupational Personality Questionnaire), all of which are based on the Big Five taxonomy. The Big Five, or Five Factor Model of normal personality, has gained acceptance since the early 1990s when some influential meta-analyses found consistent relationships between the Big Five personality factors and important criterion variables.

Disorders- At various times in history, deviant behavior has been attributed to supernatural sources, biological causes, and psychodynamic factors. The vulnerability-stress model is currently a popular way to understand the interacting personal, biological, and environmental causes of behavior.

Anxiety- We all experience anxiety, the states of tension and apprehension that is a natural response to perceived threat. In anxiety disorders, the frequency and intensity of anxiety responses are out of proportion to the situations that trigger them, and the anxiety interferes with daily life.

Anxiety responses have four components: a **subjective-emotional component**, including feelings of tension and apprehension; a **cognitive component**, including worrisome thoughts and a sense of inability to cope; **physiological responses**, including increased heart rate and blood pressure, muscle tension, and rapid breathing; and **behavioral responses**, such as avoidance of certain situations and impaired task performance.

a) **Generalized Anxiety Disorder-** A chronic (ongoing) state of diffuse, or free-floating, anxiety that is not attached to specific situations or objects. This anxiety may last for months with the signs almost continually present.

b) **Posttraumatic Stress Disorder (PTSD)-** A severe anxiety disorder that can occur in people who have been exposed to traumatic life events.

c) **Panic Disorder-** Panic attacks occur suddenly and unpredictably, and are very intense.

d) **Phobias-** Strong and irrational fears of certain objects or situations. Among the most common phobias in Western society are agoraphobia, a fear of open or public places from which escape would be difficult; social phobias, excessive fear of situations in which the person might be evaluated and possibly embarrassed; and specific phobias such as fear of dogs, snakes, spiders, airplanes, etc.

e) **Obsessive Compulsive Disorder-** Such disorders usually consist of two components-one cognitive, the other behavioral-although either can occur alone. **Obsessions** are repetitive and unwelcome thoughts, images, or impulses that invade consciousness, are often abhorrent to the person, and are very difficult to dismiss or control. **Compulsions** are repetitive behavioral responses that can be resisted only with great difficulty. Compulsions are often responses that function to reduce the anxiety associated with the intrusive thoughts.

Mood Disorders- Mood disorders are characterized by depression, mania, or both. Together with anxiety disorders, mood disorders are the most frequently experienced psychological disorders.

There is a high comorbidity involving anxiety and mood disorders.

a) **Major Depression and Causes-** In clinical depression the frequency, intensity, and duration of depressive symptoms are out of proportion to the person's life situation. Some people may respond to a minor setback or loss with major depression, an intense depressed state that leaves them unable to function effectively in their lives. Depression has four sets of symptoms: emotional, cognitive, motivational, and somatic. The symptoms of negative emotions and thoughts, loss of motivation, and behavioral slowness are reversed in mania. Both genetic and neurochemical factors have been linked to depression. One prominent biochemical theory links depression to an underactivity of the neurotransmitters (norepinephrine, dopamine, and serotonin) that activate brain areas involved in pleasure and positive motivation. Bipolar disorder seems to have an even stronger genetic component than unipolar depression.

b) **Bipolar Disorders-** When a person experiences only depression, the disorder is called unipolar depression. In a bipolar disorder, depression (which is usually the dominant state) alternates with periods of mania, a state of highly excited mood and behavior that is quite the opposite of depression. In a manic state, mood is euphoric and cognitions are grandiose. The person sees no limits to what he or she can accomplish and fails to consider negative consequences that may ensue if grandiose plans are acted on. At a motivational level, manic behavior is hyperactive.

Personality Disorders- Personality disorders are rigid, maladaptive patterns of behavior that persist over a long period of time. Personality disorders are characterized by patterns of behavior of thinking that are clearly and substantially inconsistent with the expectations of one's culture.

a) **Antisocial Personality Disorder (APD)-** People with antisocial personality disorder seem to lack a conscience, they exhibit little anxiety or guilt and tend to be impulsive and unable to delay gratification of their needs. People with APD are among the most interpersonally destructive and emotionally harmful individuals. APD is characterized by an egocentric and manipulative tendency toward immediate self-gratification, a lack of empathy for others, a tendency to act out impulsively, and a failure to profit from punishment.

b) **Narcissistic Personality Disorder-** A narcissistic personality needs undue admiration and praise, is pre-occupied with fantasies of success, accomplishment, and recognition, feels entitled to special treatment, and lacks empathy for others.

c) **Borderline Personality Disorder (BPD)-** Refers to a collection of symptoms characterized by serious instability in behavior, emotions, identity, and interpersonal relationships. A central feature of BPD is emotional dysregulation, an inability to control negative emotions in response to stressful life events, often caused by the borderline individuals themselves.

d) **Paranoid Personality Disorder-** This personality disorder is characterized by extremely suspicious and distrustful behavior. However, it is not as delusional as often found in paranoid schizophrenia.

Drug Abuse and Addiction- There are various biological and psycho-social factors that help to initiate substance abuse in an individual. Research has determined that environment and genetics can play huge roles in deciding susceptibility to addiction. The breakdown of environment and genetic factors shows that gender, ethnicity, and social class play a part in addiction development.

a) **Biological Influences-** A variety of biological factors influence drug abuse and addiction including: family history, genetic predisposition, a preexisting psychiatric or personality disorder, or a medical disorder. It is widely believed among researchers that alcoholism may be inherited. Research studies have shown that people coming from a family history of alcoholism are more likely to develop an alcohol addiction themselves. The same proves true with any other addiction such as drugs. Emotional and mental disorders have both been found to be underlying causes of addiction. Many of these are inherited, which proves how much biological and genetic makeup can influence the development of addiction.

b) **Cultural Influences-** That old question "nature or nurture?" might be better rephrased "nature and nurture" because research shows that individual health is the result of dynamic interactions between genes and environmental conditions. Environmental influences, such as exposure to drugs or stress, can alter both gene expression and gene function. In some cases, these effects may persist throughout a person's life. Research suggests that genes can also influence how a person responds to his or her environment, placing some individuals at higher risk than others. Sociocultural beliefs can shape the approach to and behavior regarding substance use and abuse. Culture plays a central role in forming the expectations of individuals about potential problems they may face with drug use. Initiation into excessive substance use may occur during periods of rapid social change, often among cultural groups who have had little exposure to the substance and who have not developed protective normative behavior.

Dissociative Identity Disorder- Dissociative disorders involve a breakdown of normal personality integration, resulting in significant alterations in memory or identity. In Dissociative Identity Disorder (DID), formerly called multiple personality disorder, two or more separate personalities coexist in the same person. DID is the most striking and widely publicized of the dissociative disorders.

Schizophrenia- Includes severe disturbances in thinking, speech, perception, emotion, and behavior. It features disordered thinking and language, poor contact with reality, flat, blunted, or inappropriate emotion, and disordered behavior. The cognitive portion of the disorder can involve delusions (false beliefs) or hallucinations (false perceptions). There are four major subtypes of schizophrenia:

a) **Paranoid-** Whose most prominent features are delusions of persecution, in which people believe that others mean to harm them, and delusions of grandeur, in which they believe they are enormously important.

b) **Disorganized-** Whose central features are confusion and incoherence, together with severe deterioration of adaptive behavior, such as personal hygiene, social skills, and self-care.

c) **Catatonic-** Characterized by striking motor disturbances ranging from muscular rigidity to random or repetitive movements.

d) **Undifferentiated-** A category assigned to people who exhibit some of the symptoms and thought disorders of the above listed categories but who do not have enough of the specific criteria to be diagnosed in those categories.

Strong evidence suggests that a genetic predisposition to schizophrenia make some people particularly vulnerable to stressful life events. The dopamine hypothesis states that schizophrenia involves over-activity of the dopamine system, resulting in too much stimulation. Some theories focus on the thought disorder that is central in schizophrenia. Deficiencies may also exist in the executive functions needed to organize behavior. Stressful life events often precede a schizophrenic episode. Studies show a higher incidence of schizophrenia at lower socioeconomic levels.

Approaches to Therapy- The basic goal of all psychotherapy, whatever the approach, is to help people change maladaptive thoughts, feelings, and behavior patterns, so that they can live happier and more productive lives.

a) **Biological Treatment-** This is a medical approach designed to alter the brain's functioning. **Drugs** have revolutionized the treatment of many behavior disorders and have permitted many hospitalized patients to function outside of institutions. Dugs that affect mood, thought, and behavior are now the most frequently prescribed medications in the United States. Effective drug treatments exist for anxiety, schizophrenia, and depression. Some of these have undesirable side effects and can be addictive. All of them affect specific classes of neurotransmitters within the brain. **Psychosurgery** refers to surgical procedures that remove or destroy brain tissue in an attempt to change disordered behavior. These techniques have become more precise, but they are still generally used only after all other treatment options have failed. **Electroconvulsive therapy (ECT)** is used primarily to treat severe depression, particularly when a threat of suicide exists. ECT, formerly known as electroshock therapy, is a standard psychiatric treatment in which seizures are electrically induced in patients to provide relief from psychiatric illnesses. ECT is usually used as a last line of intervention for major depressive disorder, schizophrenia, mania and catatonia.

b) **Psychodynamic Therapy-** The goal of psychoanalysis is to help individuals achieve insight into the conscious awareness of the psychodynamics that underlie their problems, so that they can deal adaptively with the current environment. The chief means of promoting insight into psychoanalysis are the therapist's interpretations of free associations, dream content, resistance, and transference reactions. Psychodynamic theories tend to focus more on current life events. Interpersonal theory is a structured therapy that focuses on current interpersonal problems and the development of needed interpersonal skills.

c) **Behavior Therapy-** Behavioral treatments based on classical conditioning are directed at modifying emotional responses. Exposure is designed to extinguish anxiety reactions, by exposing individuals to anxiety-arousing stimuli and preventing an avoidance response. Systematic desensitization is designed to gradually condition a response to anxiety-arousing stimuli that is incompatible with anxiety, such as relaxation. Aversion therapy is used to establish a conditioned response to an inappropriate stimulus so that it is no longer attractive. Operant procedures have been applied successfully in many behavior modification programs. Modeling is an important component of social skills training programs, which help people learn and rehearse more effective social behaviors.

d) **Cognitive Therapy-** Ellis's rational-emotive therapy and Beck's cognitive therapy focus on discovering and changing maladaptive beliefs and logical errors of thinking that underlie maladaptive emotional responses and behaviors.

e) **Humanistic and Existential Therapy-** Attempts to liberate people's natural tendency toward self-actualization, by establishing a growth-inducing therapeutic relationship. Roger's person-centered therapy emphasizes the importance of three therapist characteristics: unconditional positive regard, empathy, and genuineness. The goal of Gestalt therapy is to remove blockages to people's awareness of the wholeness of immediate experience, by making them more aware of their feelings and the ways in which they interact with others.

f) **Family and Couples Therapy-** Family therapy is based on the notion that individuals' problems are often reflections of dysfunctional family systems. It is thought that such systems should be treated as a unit. Marital therapies help couples improve their communication patterns and resolve difficulties in their relationships. In behavioral marital therapies, couples receive communication and relations skills training to increase positive interactions in their marriages.

Unit Ten Practice Quiz

1. Margo exhibits a lack of conscience and a total disregard for human life and emotion. She may be showing symptoms of:
   A) Narcissistic personality disorder
   B) Borderline personality disorder
   C) Bipolar disorder
   D) Antisocial personality disorder

2. True or False: Emotion-focused coping involves treating a situation head-on at the source in order to reduce stress.
   A) True
   B) False

3. Which of the following is NOT a phase of the general adaption syndrome?
   A) Alarm
   B) Resolve
   C) Exhaustion
   D) Resistance

4. True or False: Obsessions are repetitive and unwanted thoughts that are difficult to control.
   A) True
   B) False

5. All of the following are subtypes of schizophrenia EXCEPT:
   A) Undifferentiated
   B) Paranoid
   C) Catatonic
   D) Monocular

6. Electroconvulsive therapy (ECT) is primarily used to treat:
   A) Depression
   B) Anxiety
   C) PTSD
   D) Serotonin syndrome

7. True or False: An associative strategy of control may include distracting oneself from a painful sensory input.
   A) True
   B) False

8. Which of the following might be an example of a social phobia?
   A) Sitting on a busy train
   B) Groups of spiders
   C) Airplanes
   D) Eating

Answer Key: 1=D, 2=B, 3=B, 4=A, 5=D, 6=A, 7=B, 8=A

Unit Eleven: Social Psychology

Learning Objectives
After completing this unit, you should be able to:

1. Discuss what factors influence conformity
2. Discuss how we form attributions
3. Discuss how we form impressions
4. Describe how attitudes and behavior are related
5. Discuss what factors influence group behavior
6. Discuss what causes prejudice
7. Discuss what measures can be used to measure prejudice
8. Discuss steps to help reduce prejudice and discrimination

Behavior in Social and Cultural Context
Social psychology is the study of how the behavior of individuals is influenced by other people. This field is commonly broken into three areas: social cognition, social influence, and social relationships.

Social Roles- Consist of a set of norms that characterizes how people in a given social position ought to behave. Social norms are shared expectations about how people should think, feel, and behave, and they are the glue that binds social systems together. Norms and roles can influence behavior so strongly that they compel a person to act uncharacteristically.

   a) **Milgram's Obedience Study-** This famous research study was known as Milgram's experiments or obedience experiments. Each study was descriptive in which all participants were exposed to the same situations and were observed under controlled laboratory conditions. Milgram, however, carefully changed (manipulated) different aspects of the situations, from one study to another, in order to identify factors that increased or decreased people's obedience. The Milgram experiments on obedience to authority figures were a series of social psychology experiments. They measured the willingness of study participants to obey an authority figure who instructed them to perform acts conflicting with their personal conscience. He had examined justifications for acts of genocide offered by those accused at the World War II, Nuremberg War Criminal trials. Their defense often was based on "obedience" - that they were just following the orders of their superiors. For his study, volunteers were recruited to investigate "learning" (re: ethics: deception). At the beginning, a volunteer was introduced to another participant, who was actually a confederate of the experimenter (Milgram). The volunteer was designated a "teacher" and the confederate a "learner". The "learner" was strapped to a chair with electrodes. After he had learned a given list of word pairs, the "teacher" tested him. The teacher was told to administer an electric shock every time the learner made a mistake, increasing the level of shock each time. The conclusion of the study indicated that ordinary people are likely to follow orders given by an authority figure, even to the extent of killing an innocent human being. Obedience to authority is ingrained in us all from the way we are brought up. People tend to obey orders from other people if they recognize their authority as morally right and / or legally based. This response to legitimate authority is learned in a variety of situations, for example, in the family, school and workplace.

b) **Zimbardo's Prison Study-** The Stanford prison experiment (SPE) was a study of the psychological effects of becoming a prisoner or prison guard. The experiment was conducted at Stanford University, August 14–20, 1971, by a team of researchers led by psychology professor Philip Zimbardo. It was funded by the US Office of Naval Research and was of interest to both the US Navy and Marine Corps, as an investigation into the causes of conflict between military guards and prisoners. Twenty-four male students out of seventy-five were selected to take on randomly assigned roles of prisoners and guards, in a mock prison situated in the basement of the Stanford psychology building. The participants adapted to their roles well beyond Zimbardo's expectations, as the guards enforced authoritarian measures and ultimately subjected some of the prisoners to psychological torture. Many of the prisoners passively accepted psychological abuse and, at the request of the guards, readily harassed other prisoners who attempted to prevent it. The experiment even affected Zimbardo himself, who, in his role as the superintendent, permitted the abuse to continue. Two of the prisoners quit the experiment early and the entire experiment was abruptly stopped after only six days. Certain portions of the experiment were filmed and excerpts of footage are publicly available. The results of the experiment favor situational attribution of behavior rather than dispositional attribution (a result caused by internal characteristics). In other words, it seemed that the situation, rather than their individual personalities, caused the participants' behavior. Under this interpretation, the results are compatible with the results of the Milgram experiment, in which ordinary people fulfilled orders to administer what appeared to be agonizing and dangerous electric shocks to a confederate of the experimenter.

c) **Why People Obey-** Social norms are shared expectations about how group members should behave. People conform because of informational and normative social influence. The majority's size and presence of a dissenter influence people's degree of conformity. Milgram's research found an unexpectedly high percentage of people willing to obey destructive orders. Such obedience is stronger when the victim is remote and when the authority figure is close by, legitimate, and assumes responsibility for what happens. The results of Milgram's and Zimbardo's studies provide examples of how social contexts can induce people to behave in ways they never would have imagined possible. Some of the pressures to influence a person's behavior come in the form of deliberate strategies. By learning to identify these techniques, people will be in a better position to resist them. The **powerful norm of reciprocity** involves the expectation that when others treat us well, we should respond in kind. The **door-in-the-face technique** is when a persuader makes a large request, expecting it to be rejected, and the presents a smaller request. The **foot-in-the-door technique** is when a persuader first gets compliance with a small request and then later presents a larger request. The final technique is low balling, where a persuader gets a person to commit to an action, and then before actually performing the action they increase the cost of that same behavior. By recognizing what compliance techniques are being used to manipulate behavior, people are in a better position to resist them.

Social Cognition- Refers to how we process information about other people. This process involves three key aspects of social thinking: attributions, impressions, and attitudes. Attributions are judgments about the causes of our own and other people's behavior and outcomes.

a) **Attribution Theory-** Deals with the types of explanations people generate for other's behavior and how those explanations come about. There are two types of attributions (explanations of behavior) that a person could come up with. **Dispositional (or internal) attributions** explain behavior in terms of factors inside the person (personality, intelligence, maturity, and so forth). **Situational (or external) attributions** explain behavior in terms of factors outside the person (such as luck, interference from other people, social etiquette). Consistency, distinctiveness, and consensus information jointly influences whether we make personal or situational attributions for behavior. We often underestimate the role of situational factors when making attributions for other people's behavior, and we display a self-serving bias when making attributions for our own successes and failures.

b) **Fundamental Attribution Error-** Social psychology teaches us that the immediate social environment profoundly influences behavior, yet at times we ignore this when making attributions. Instead, we commit a bias called the fundamental attribution error: we underestimate the impact of the situation and overestimate the role of personal factors when explaining other people's behavior. When people have time to reflect on their judgments or are highly motivated to be careful, the fundamental attribution error is reduced. The fundamental attribution error applies to how we perceive other people's behavior, not our own.

c) **Self-serving Bias-** When it comes to explaining our own behavior, we often make attributions that protect or enhance our self-esteem by displaying a self-serving bias, the tendency to make personal attributions for successes and situational attributions for failures.

d) **Just-world Hypothesis-** Or just-world fallacy, is the cognitive bias (or assumption) that a person's actions always bring morally fair and fitting consequences to that person; so that all noble actions are eventually rewarded and all evil actions are eventually punished. In other words, the just-world hypothesis is the tendency to attribute consequences to or expect consequences as the result of a universal force that restores moral balance. The fallacy is that this implies (often unintentionally) the existence of cosmic justice, destiny, divine providence, deserts, stability, or order, and may also serve to rationalize people's misfortune on the grounds that they deserve it.

Attitudes and Attitude Change- Beyond attributions and impressions, much of our social thinking involves attitudes that we hold. An attitude is a positive or negative evaluative reaction toward a stimulus, such as a person, action, object, or concept. Our attitudes help define our identity, guide our actions, and influence how we judge people. First impressions generally carry extra weight. Stereotypes and schemas create perceptual sets that shape our impressions. Through self-fulfilling prophecies, our initially false expectations shape the way we act toward someone. In turn, this person responds to our behavior in ways that confirm our expectations.

First, attitudes influence behavior more strongly when situational factors that contradict our attitudes are weak. According to the theory of planned behavior, our intention to engage in a behavior is strongest when we have a positive attitude toward that behavior, when subjective norms (our perceptions of what other people think we should do) support our attitudes, and we believe that the behavior is under our control. Second, attitudes have a greater influence on behavior when we are aware of them and when they are strongly held. Third, general attitudes best predict general classes of behavior, and specific attitudes best predict specific behaviors.

Attitudes predict behavior best when situational influences are weak, when the attitude is strong, and when we consciously think about our attitude. Behavior also influences attitudes. Counterattitudinal behavior is where a person behaves in a way that is inconsistent with their attitudes. This is most likely to create cognitive dissonance (an unpleasant state of tension) when the behavior is feely chosen and threatens self-worth, or produces foreseeable negative consequences. To reduce dissonance, we may change our attitude to become more consistent with how we have acted. The self-perception theory also helps promote attitude change, where we make inferences about our own attitudes in much the same way by observing how we behave.

Persuasion represents the intersection of social thinking and social influence. In persuasion, communicator credibility is highest when the communicator is perceived as expert and trustworthy. Fear-arousing communications may be effective if they arouse moderate to strong fear and suggest how to avoid the feared result. The central route to persuasion occurs when people think carefully about the message and are influenced because they find the arguments compelling. It works best with listeners who have a high need for cognition. For those with a low cognition need, the peripheral route works better. This occurs when people do not scrutinize the message but are influenced mostly by other factors such as a speaker's attractiveness or a message's emotional appeal.

Group Behavior- Much of human behavior occurs in groups. People often form groups to share interests and activities and to perform tasks and achieve goals that are too complex or demanding to be accomplished by one person.

  a) **Asch's Study on Conformity-** In psychology, the Asch conformity experiments, or the Asch Paradigm, were a series of laboratory experiments, directed by Solomon Asch in the 1950s, that demonstrated the degree to which an individual's own opinions are influenced by those of a majority group. Each participant was placed in a room with seven confederates. Confederates were introduced as participants to the real participant. Participants were shown a card with a line on it, followed by a card with three lines of different lengths, labeled A, B, and C, respectively. Participants were then asked to say aloud which line (A, B, or C) matched the length of the line on the first card. Each line question was called a "trial". For the first two trials, the participant would feel at ease, as he and the confederates gave the obvious, correct answer. On the third trial, the confederates would all give the same wrong answer, placing the participant in a dilemma. There were 18 trials in total and the confederates answered incorrectly for 12 of them. These 12 were known as critical trials. The aim was to see whether or not the real participant would change his answers to agree with the confederates' incorrect answers. Through analysis of participants' responses, Asch discovered that there were vast individual differences in reaction to the experimental situation. Over one-third gave incorrect answers. Interview data revealed that even participants who did not conform to the majority group — and thus remained independent from the group — reacted to the experiment in different ways. Some reacted with confidence in their perception and experience. Despite experiencing conflict between their idea of the correct answer and the group's incorrect answer; they stuck with the answer that was based on their own perception. Behavior in the Asch study is an example of **normative social influence**: pressure to comply with a norm (even one that is obviously wrong) coming from concern about being rejected by the group. In ambiguous situations, where there are no known norms and no clear basis for deciding how to behave, people often react to **informational social influence;** what other people do simply provides information about how to behave.

  b) **Groupthink-** The tendency of group members to suspend critical thinking because they are striving to seek agreement. Groupthink is most likely to occur when a group is under high pressure to reach a decision, is insulated from outside input, has a leader who promotes a personal agenda, and has high cohesiveness, reflecting a spirit of closeness and ability to work well together. **Social loafing** is the tendency for people to expend less individual effort when working in a group than when working alone. Key decisions are often entrusted to groups, such as committees, because groups are assumed to be more conservative than individuals. If group members lean toward a liberal or risky viewpoint to begin with, the group's decision will tend to become more liberal or riskier. This principle is called **group polarization**: when a group of like-minded people discuss an issue, the average opinion of group members tends to become more extreme. In crowds, people may experience deindividuation, a loss of individuality that leads to disinhibited behavior.

c) **Diffusion of Responsibility-** Is a sociopsychological phenomenon whereby a person is less likely to take responsibility for action or inaction when others are present. Considered a form of attribution, the individual assumes that others either are responsible for taking action or have already done so. The phenomenon tends to occur in groups of people above a certain critical size and when responsibility is not explicitly assigned. It rarely occurs when the person is alone; diffusion increases with groups of three or more. Diffusion of responsibility occurs in large group settings and under both prosocial and antisocial conditions. In prosocial situations, individuals' willingness to intervene or assist someone in need is inhibited by the presence of other people. The individual believes that other people present will or should intervene. Thus, the individual does not perceive it as his or her responsibility to take action. In antisocial situations, negative behaviors are more likely to be carried out when the person is in a group of similarly motivated individuals.

The behavior is driven by the deindividuating effects of group membership, and the diffusion of feelings of personal responsibility for the consequences. As part of this process, individuals become less self-aware and feel an increased sense of anonymity. As a result, they are less likely to feel responsible for any antisocial behavior performed by their group. Diffusion of responsibility can manifest itself in a group of people who, through action or inaction, allow events to occur which they would never allow if they were alone. Groupthink and groupshift is where a group of people working on a task lose motivation, feel less responsibility for achievement of group goals, and hide their lack of effort in the group (social loafing). It applies in hierarchical organizations when subordinates claim to be simply following orders, and supervisors claim that they merely issue directives and do not perform the actions under question. The difficulty of identifying the culpable party is often seen in trials regarding crimes against humanity.

d) **Altruism-** Is behavior aimed at unselfishly helping others and is the principle or practice of concern for the welfare of others. It is a traditional virtue in many cultures and a core aspect of various religious traditions and secular worldviews, though the concept of "others" toward whom concern should be directed, can vary among cultures and religions. Altruism or selflessness is the opposite of selfishness. Altruism can be distinguished from feelings of loyalty. Pure altruism consists of sacrificing something for someone other than the self (e.g. sacrificing time, energy or possessions) with no expectation of any compensation or benefits, either direct, or indirect (e.g., receiving recognition for the act of giving).

Social Identities- According to social identity theory, prejudice stems from a need to enhance our self-esteem. Some experiments find that people express more prejudice after their self-esteem is threatened and that the opportunity to derogate others helps restore self-esteem.

   a) **Acculturation-** Explains the process of cultural change and psychological change that results following a meeting between cultures. The effects of acculturation can be seen at multiple levels in both interacting cultures. At the group level, acculturation often results in changes to culture, customs, and social institutions. Noticeable group level effects of acculturation often include changes in food, clothing, and language. At the individual level, differences in the way individuals acculturate have been shown to be associated, not just with changes in daily behavior, but with numerous measures of psychological and physical well-being. As enculturation is used to describe the process of first-culture learning, acculturation can be thought of as second-culture learning. Acculturation is thought to impact health by impacting levels of stress, access to health resources, and attitudes towards health. In situations of continuous contact, cultures have exchanged and blended foods, music, dances, clothing, tools, and technologies. Cultural exchange can either occur naturally through extended contact, or deliberately though cultural appropriation or cultural imperialism. In some instances, acculturation results in the adoption of another country's language, which is then modified over time to become a new, distinct, language.

   b) **Ethnocentrism-** Is judging another culture solely by the values and standards of one's own culture. Ethnocentric individuals judge other groups relative to their own ethnic group or culture, especially with regard to language, behavior, customs, and religion. These ethnic distinctions and subdivisions serve to define each ethnicity's unique cultural identity. Ethnocentrism may be overt or subtle, and while it is considered a natural proclivity of human psychology, it has developed a generally negative connotation. Ethnocentrism is a universal human reaction found in all known societies, in all groups and in practically all individuals. Everyone learns ethnocentrism while growing up. The functions of ethnocentrism in maintaining order are more apparent than those which promote social change. Ethnocentrism encourages the solidarity of the group. Believing that one's own ways are the best, encourages a "we" feeling with associates, and strengthens the idea that loyalty to comrades and preservation of the basis for superiority are important values. Positively, ethnocentrism promotes continuance of the status quo negatively, it discourages change. Ethnocentrism hinders the understanding of cooperation with other groups. If the ways of one's own group are best, there is little incentive to interact with "inferior" groups. In fact, attitudes of suspicion, disdain and hostility are likely to be engendered. Extreme ethnocentrism is likely to promote conflict, as the records of past wars, and religious and racial conflicts reveal. Conflict, of course, often leads to social change, and in that sense ethnocentrism becomes a vehicle for the promotion of social change. It does so, however, through encouragement of its peaceful evolution.

c) **Stereotypes-** Are a generalized belief about a group or category of people, and represent a powerful schema. In social psychology, a stereotype is a thought that can be adopted about specific types of individuals or certain ways of doing things. Stereotypes, prejudice, and discrimination are understood as related but different concepts. Stereotypes are regarded as the most cognitive component and often occur without conscious awareness; prejudice is the affective component of stereotyping; and discrimination is the behavioral component of prejudicial reactions. Possible prejudicial effects of stereotypes are: justification of ill-founded prejudices or ignorance; unwillingness to rethink one's attitudes and behavior toward stereotyped groups; and preventing some people of stereotyped groups from entering or succeeding in activities or fields.

Prejudice- Refers to a negative attitude toward people, based on their membership of a group. Discrimination refers to overt behavior that involves treating people unfairly based on the group to which they belong.

a) **Measuring Prejudice-** Prejudice is an adverse judgment made without knowing the relevant facts, or formation of an opinion beforehand without good justification. Sociologists do have tools which facilitate measuring prejudice. The common form is to conduct surveys with open-ended questions, like in Likert Scale surveys. The Bogardus Scale, although an old measurement tool, is still used for prejudice measurement against a certain group of people. Another tool is the Harvard's Implicit Association Test (IAT). Some contemporary measurement tools are also used these days, in addition to the written formats. Likert is a psychometric scale, commonly used in questionnaires, with different levels of agreements, against each question, for respondents. This is a widely used scale in survey research. The Bogardus Social Distance Scale empirically measures people's willingness to participate in social contacts of varying degrees of closeness with members of diverse social groups. These groups can be other races, ethnic groups, homosexuals etc. The Implicit Association Test is, however, an experimental measure within social psychology. It is designed to detect the strength of a person's automatic association between representations of concepts. The test requires rapid categorization of the target concepts with an attribute. The pairings are later studied and interpreted. The faster pairings are stronger concepts, while the slower pairing are weaker. These results measure an individual's implicit attitudes, many times even without the subject's awareness.

b) **Implicit vs. Explicit Prejudice-** Examples of overt prejudice and discrimination are abundant even in this day and age. Although prejudiced attitudes may have faded a bit, in many ways modern racism, sexism, and other forms of prejudice are more difficult to detect. In contrast to **explicit prejudice**, which people express publicly, **implicit prejudice** is hidden from public view.

c) **Reducing Prejudice-** The best known approaches to prejudice reduction are based on a principle called **equal status contact**: prejudice between people is most likely to be reduced when they engage in sustained close contact; have equal status; work to achieve a common goal that requires cooperation; and are supported by broader social norms.

Unit Eleven Practice Quiz

1. Which hypothesis explains that people are under an assumption that ultimately, good actions will be rewarded, and poor actions will be punished?
   A) Self-serving
   B) Fundamental attribution error
   C) Just-world
   D) Dispositional error

2. True or False: The door-in-the-face technique includes making a small request in order to build the other person up to accepting larger requests.
   A) True
   B) False

3. Fred experiences bouts of laziness when working in groups because he assumes that the other members will pull his weight. This is an example of:
   A) Social loafing
   B) Groupthink
   C) Bystander effect
   D) Group polarization

4. True or False: In Zimbardo's study, volunteers were recruited to administer electric shocks to "victims" who answered questions incorrectly.
   A) True
   B) False

5. Which of the following is an example of explicit prejudice?
   A) Writing judgmental thoughts in a journal
   B) Publically burning another country's flag
   C) Thinking that one race is superior to another
   D) Believing that persons outside of your gender are inferior

6. The act of sacrificing elements of oneself for the welfare of others is called:
   A) Altruism
   B) Acculturation
   C) Amicability
   D) Allocation

7. Which attribution theory explains behaviors in terms of external factors such as luck and interference from others?
   A) Situational
   B) Dispositional

8. The belief that one's own culture is superior to others is known as:
   A) Egoism
   B) Cognitive dissonance
   C) Norm of reciprocity
   D) Ethnocentrism

Answer Key: 1=C, 2=B, 3=A, 4=B, 5=B, 6=A, 7=A, 8=D

Practice Test

1. Which humanistic psychologist was a proponent of offering clients a supportive environment in which to delve into their feelings?
   A) Ivan Pavlov
   B) Carl Rogers
   C) B.F. Skinner
   D) Jean Piaget

2. Which of the following is not associated with structuralism?
   A) Introspection
   B) Wilhelm Wundt
   C) Breaking things down into basic components
   D) Emotional regulation

3. Who developed psychodynamic theory?
   A) Sigmund Freud
   B) Charles Darwin
   C) John Watson
   D) Albert Einstein

4. Which of the following sequences pertains to the humanistic perspective?
   A) Feelings, defense mechanisms, heredity
   B) Heredity, experiences, and the unconscious mind
   C) Self-actualization, freedom, personal growth
   D) Personal growth, evolution, behavior

5. What does choosing the appropriate research method depend upon?
   A) The investigator's objectives
   B) In-depth analysis
   C) The participants' feelings
   D) Social interactions

6. Which of the following is an advantage of case studies?
   A) Objectivity in the way data are gathered and interpreted
   B) Universality of findings
   C) Challenge the validity of a theory or scientific belief
   D) The researcher's subjective impressions

7. What is it called when research participants do not know whether or not they are receiving a placebo?
   A) Double blind
   B) Placebo effect
   C) Experimental study
   D) Control group

8. A researcher studies the impact of time spent watching television on a person's weight. What is the dependent variable?
   A) Time spent watching television
   B) The person's overall health
   C) The person's weight
   D) The person's motivation

9. What would be the most appropriate method for a high school student to gather data on his/her classmates' study habits?
   A) Experiment
   B) Survey
   C) Longitudinal study
   D) Informal interview

10. _____ is not associated with inferential statistics.
    A) Statistical significance
    B) Null hypothesis
    C) Alternative hypothesis
    D) Measures of central tendency

11. Which of the following is not a part of DNA molecules?
    A) Adenine
    B) Glucosamine
    C) Thymine
    D) Guanine

12. _____ is an individual's observable characteristics while _____ is their genetic makeup.
    A) Phenotype; genotype
    B) Prototype; genotype
    C) Genotype; phenotype
    D) Genotype; prototype

13. What is the purpose of the myelin sheath?
    A) To protect the dendrites
    B) To control the axon
    C) To speed up information transmission
    D) To accelerate impulse speed

14. Which of these are related to the midbrain?
    A) The right and left hemispheres
    B) The spinal cord and brain stem
    C) Language and mathematical abilities
    D) Visual and auditory perception

15. Which of the following is not related to the hypothalamus?
    A) Memory retrieval
    B) Sexual behavior
    C) Aggression
    D) Sleeping

16. The _____ operates during states of relaxation while the _____ is operates during states of arousal.
    A) Autonomic nervous system; parasympathetic
    B) Parasympathetic nervous system; sympathetic nervous system
    C) Sympathetic nervous system; parasympathetic nervous system
    D) Parasympathetic nervous system; empathic nervous system

17. What is the purpose of the rods that are found in the retina?
    A) To focus on nearby objects
    B) To allow color to be seen
    C) To focus on distant objects
    D) To help in low light environments

18. Which of the following is not located in the middle ear?
    A) Stapes
    B) Malleus
    C) Cochlea
    D) Incus

19. Which of the following are monocular cues?
    A) Texture
    B) Linear perspective
    C) Interposition
    D) All of the above

20. What grouping best describes stage two of the sleep cycle?
    A) Dreams, slower heart rate, slower breathing
    B) Delta waves, difficult in awakening, rapid brain activity
    C) Body jerks, dreams, eye movement
    D) None of the above

21. What is the purpose of the blood-brain barrier?
    A) To aid in neurotransmitter stimulation
    B) To inhibit neurotransmitter activity
    C) To help store synthesized neurotransmitters
    D) To screen out foreign substances

22. Which of the following is not a depressant?
    A) Barbiturates
    B) Morphine
    C) Alcohol
    D) Tranquilizers

23. How is substance dependence defined?
    A) A pattern that develops during which an individual's body produces compensatory responses to counteract a drug's effect
    B) A pattern that develops during which an individual experiences withdrawal symptoms
    C) A pattern that develops during which an individual's life is substantially impaired
    D) A pattern that develops during which an individual experiences an increase in intensity of a drug's effect

24. What are typical characteristics of opiates?
    A) Relaxation, decreased heart rate, slower body functions
    B) Heightened sensory experiences, hallucinations, euphoric feelings
    C) Pain relief, mood changes, highly addictive
    D) Mood changes, anxiety relief, sensory distortions

25. Nadia screamed when she was stung by a bee. Now, when she hears one buzzing, the screams. Her scream is considered to be a(n) _____.
    A) Conditioned response
    B) Unconditioned stimulus
    C) Conditioned stimulus
    D) Unconditioned response

26. Who is associated with operant conditioning?
    A) Thorndike
    B) Skinner
    C) Pavlov
    D) Bandura

27. What is not linked to confabulation?
    A) Alzheimer's disease
    B) Aneurysms
    C) Dementia
    D) Parkinson's disease

28. Which of the following is not related to memory?
    A) Retrieval
    B) Storage
    C) Encoding
    D) None of the above

29. How are mnemonic devices helpful?
    A) They help individuals to elaborate on a subject
    B) They help individuals to retrieve information from short-term memory
    C) They help individuals to retrieve information from long-term memory
    D) They allow individuals to create cues

30. What is a benefit of using continuous reinforcement?
    A) More rapid learning
    B) Consequences are easier to perceive
    C) Behaviors are more readily associated with consequences
    D) All of the above

31. When food and water are used as reinforcers, they are referred to as _____.
    A) Tertiary
    B) Primary
    C) Secondary
    D) Basic

32. What is another name for instincts?
    A) Fixed action patterns
    B) Automatic responses
    C) Primal urges
    D) Fixed behavioral patterns

33. Which of the following is not associated with bulimia nervosa?
    A) Poor impulse control
    B) Lack of personal identity
    C) High achievement
    D) Anxiety

34. About how much do genetic factors account for variation in body mass index among men and women?
    A) 20-40%
    B) 40-70%
    C) 30-50%
    D) None of the above

35. What is the correct order of the human physiological response pattern to sexual intercourse?
    A) Plateau phase, excitement phase, resolution phase, orgasm phase
    B) Excitement phase, orgasm phase, resolution phase, plateau phase
    C) Excitement phase, plateau phase, orgasm phase, resolution phase
    D) Orgasm phase, excitement phase, plateau phase, resolution phase

36. According to Maslow, what is the ultimate human motive and at the top of the hierarchy of needs?
    A) Self-actualization
    B) Self-efficacy
    C) Self-love
    D) Self-esteem

37. Where do negative emotions seem to elicit the most activation?
    A) Right hemisphere
    B) Left hemisphere
    C) Amygdala
    D) Limbic system

38. What does the Cannon-Bard theory propose?
    A) That we first become aroused and then judge what we are feeling
    B) That arousal and cognition are independent are both triggered by the thalamus
    C) That arousal tells us how strongly we are feeling
    D) That situational cues help us label specific emotions

39. Display rules are cultural depictions of how emotions are to be expressed.
    A) True
    B) False

40. Which of the following does a polygraph test not measure?
    A) Skin conductance
    B) Heart rate
    C) Respiration
    D) None of the above

41. Which of the following is not associated with emotions?
    A) Influence how others behave towards us
    B) Social communication
    C) Spiritual fulfillment
    D) Preparation for how events impact our lives

42. Which of the following terms best describes the mental framework of the world humans build?
    A) Concepts
    B) Schema
    C) Prototypes
    D) Memory

43. What is the main difference between the subconscious mind and the unconscious mind?
    A) The unconscious consists of accessible information, while the subconscious consists of primitive information
    B) The subconscious consists of accessible information, while the unconscious mind consists of inaccessible information
    C) The subconscious consists of awareness in the present moment, while the unconscious mind consists of inaccessible information
    D) None of the above

44. Which of the following biases is based on the notion of people being intrinsically motivated to do the right thing?
    A) Confirmation bias
    B) Avoiding loss bias
    C) Fairness bias
    D) Hindsight bias

45. _____ describes feelings of discomfort that result from when a person holds two conflicting beliefs.
    A) Cognitive dissonance
    B) Cognitive disparity
    C) Cognitive duality
    D) Cognitive discrepancy

46. What does misattribution refer to?
    A) The inability to express a feeling
    B) Difficulty in recognizing others
    C) Making a mistaken assumption as to what caused a feeling
    D) Making an assumption about how others feel

47. What are the three standards for psychological tests?
    A) Measurement, reliability, consistency
    B) Intelligence quotient, aptitude, achievement
    C) Validity, standardization, intelligence
    D) Reliability, standardization, validity

48. What is metacognition?
    A) Processes used to plan and regulate task performance
    B) The diverse forms of intelligence
    C) Awareness of one's emotions
    D) Regulation of one's emotional response

49. Which heuristic involves forming smaller steps in order to reach a bigger goal?
    A) Means-end
    B) Availability
    C) Subgoal
    D) Approach

50. Which kind of reasoning entails back-and-forth conversations?
    A) Deductive
    B) Dialectical
    C) Subconscious
    D) Inductive

51. Which of the following describes how a child may behave during the Piaget's preoperational stage?
    A) A child thinking that a ball disappeared when it rolled out of sight
    B) A child holding a conversation with an adult
    C) A child pretending to be dog
    D) A child performing mathematical computations

52. Which of the following is not an assumption of Vygotsky's theory?
    A) Individuals can think logically about concrete and abstract problems
    B) Complex mental activities begin as basic social activities
    C) Children can perform more difficult tasks with a more advanced individual
    D) Children develop through informal and formal conversations with adults

53. When does Erikson's initiative v. guilt stage of development occur?
    A) Ages 1-2
    B) Ages 6-puberty
    C) Ages 3-5
    D) During the first year

54. Why is Erikson's intimacy v. isolation stage important?
    A) Because it allows individuals to be introspective
    B) Because it is marked by the ability to form lasting and meaningful relationships
    C) Because it is marked by the ability to care for others
    D) Because it encourages people to strive to do well

55. What did Kohlberg's theory pertain to?
   A) Psychosocial development
   B) Moral development
   C) Sociocultural development
   D) Cognitive development

56. Choose the correct sequence of prenatal development.
   A) Embryonic, zygote, germinal, fetus
   B) Fetus, embryonic, zygote, germinal
   C) Germinal, zygote, embryonic, fetus
   D) Zygote, embryonic, fetus, germinal

57. About when does separation anxiety typically appear in children?
   A) 6-7 months of age
   B) 7-8 months of age
   C) 10-12 months of age
   D) 12-16 months of age

58. What is a morpheme?
   A) The smallest unit of meaning in language
   B) An opiate
   C) The smallest unit of speech sound
   D) The smallest unit of language

59. Which chromosome combination would result in a female offspring?
   A) X
   B) XY
   C) XX
   D) XYX

60. Which of the following is not considered a teratogen?
   A) Drugs
   B) Environmental toxins
   C) Maternal illness
   D) None of the above

61. What is not a characteristic of adolescence?
    A) The search for identity
    B) The increasing importance of peer relationships
    C) The preparation for marriage transition
    D) The improvement of information processing abilities

62. Children are born with specific attachment behavior.
    A) True
    B) False

63. What is one difference between the ego and the id?
    A) The ego functions on a conscious level while the id functions in an irrational manner
    B) The ego functions on a moral level while the id functions on a basic level
    C) The ego functions around values and ideals while the id functions around basic needs
    D) The ego functions around the pleasure principle while the id functions on reality

64. Which of the following defense mechanisms is described as a repressed impulse released in the form of a socially acceptable or admired behavior?
    A) Projection
    B) Displacement
    C) Sublimation
    D) Reaction formation

65. What is the correct order of Freud's psychosexual stages?
    A) Oral, phallic, anal, latency, genital
    B) Anal, oral, latency, phallic, genital
    C) Phallic, anal, latency, oral, genital
    D) Oral, anal, phallic, latency, genital

66. According to Freud, during which stage can the Oedipus and Electra complexes appear?
    A) Anal
    B) Phallic
    C) Oral
    D) Genital

67. How would Jung describe archetypes?
    A) Memories accumulated throughout the entire history of the human race
    B) An individual's main enemy
    C) An unconscious based on a person's life experiences
    D) Inherited tendencies to interpret experiences in certain ways

68. According to Carl Rogers, what is self-verification?
    A) The need to confirm the self-concept and change
    B) The highest realization of human potential
    C) How positively or negatively individuals feel about themselves
    D) A strong and pervasive tendency to gain and preserve a positive self-image

69. What is vicarious reinforcement?
    A) Social learning that occurs through observation of rewards and punishments
    B) Social learning that occurs through rewards and punishments
    C) Social learning that occurs when one wants to live like another person
    D) Social learning that occurs through trial and error

70. What is the term used to describe how a person's behavior, environment, and personal qualities influence one another?
    A) Reciprocal functioning
    B) Reciprocal determinism
    C) Cultural reciprocity
    D) Reciprocity

71. Which of the following is not a part of the Eysenck's Big Five personality traits?
    A) Neuroticism
    B) Openness
    C) Conscientiousness
    D) None of the above

72. Which of the following is not a crucial element of learning?
    A) Reproduction
    B) Motivation
    C) Closure
    D) Retention

73. What happens during the resistance phase of the general adaptation syndrome (GAS)?
    A) The sympathetic nervous system is activated
    B) The body may become vulnerable to diseases
    C) The endocrine system releases stress hormones
    D) The body may exhibit physiological arousal

For the next four questions, please choose the best matching answer regarding the DSM-IV-TR classification system.

74. Axis I   A) Psychosocial or environmental problems
75. Axis IV   B) Current clinical symptoms
76. Axis III   C) Personality disorders or mental retardation
77. Axis II   D) Medical conditions

78. Why do researchers and clinicians use projective testing with participants/clients?
    A) Because it lends support about people's tendency to project their issues onto others
    B) Because it may provide researchers with important internal processes about their subjects
    C) Because it is easily accessible and interpreted
    D) Because it is not necessary for one to be trained in order to administer the tests

79. Which of the following is not an objective test?
    A) Rorschach test
    B) MMPI
    C) BDI
    D) Child behavior checklist

80. Which of the following is not a component of anxiety responses?
    A) Cognitive component
    B) Physiological component
    C) Subjective-emotional component
    D) Vulnerability-stress component

81. What are compulsions?
    A) Repetitive and unwelcomed thoughts, images, or impulses
    B) Repetitive thoughts that invade one's consciousness
    C) Repetitive behavioral responses that reduce anxiety
    D) Repetitive behavioral responses that increase anxiety

82. What is the most frequently experienced psychological disorder?
    A) Anxiety
    B) Personality disorders
    C) Mood disorders
    D) A and C

83. A biochemical theory links depression to the _____ of norepinephrine, dopamine, and serotonin.
    A) Overproduction
    B) Underproduction
    C) Underactivity
    D) Overactivity

84. What is bipolar disorder?
    A) Another name for a depressive state
    B) Periods of mania and depression
    C) Multiple personality disorder
    D) None of the above

85. Which of the following is not a characteristic of antisocial personality disorder?
    A) An inability to control negative emotions in response to stressful events
    B) A tendency towards immediate self-gratification
    C) A lack of empathy for others
    D) A failure to profit from punishment

86. Personality disorders are rigid, maladaptive patterns of behavior that persist over a long period of time.
    A) True
    B) False

87. Emotional and mental disorders are not underlying causes of addiction.
    A) True
    B) False

88. What subtype of schizophrenia is marked by confusion, incoherence, and the deterioration of adaptive behaviors?
    A) Undifferentiated
    B) Catatonic
    C) Disorganized
    D) Paranoid

89. Electroconvulsive therapy (ECT) is used primarily to treat what kind of issues?
    A) Addiction and bipolar disorders
    B) DID and depression
    C) Anxiety and insomnia
    D) Depression and schizophrenia

90. What is aversion therapy?
    A) A form of social modeling that help individuals learn more effective social behaviors
    B) Used to establish a conditioned response to an inappropriate stimulus so that it is no longer attractive
    C) Used to gradually condition a response to anxiety-arousing stimuli that is incompatible with anxiety
    D) Used to expose individuals to anxiety-arousing stimuli to prevent an avoidance response

91. What are the therapist characteristics of which Rogers emphasized the importance?
    A) Self-actualization, unconditional positive regard, experience
    B) Positivity, friendliness, openness
    C) Empathy, unconditional positive regard, genuineness
    D) Genuineness, non-judgmental attitude, communication

92. Which of the following is an example of a social phobia?
    A) Sitting on a crowded bus
    B) Eating alone
    C) Supermarkets
    D) Heights

93. What two names are associated with experiments of social norms and obedience?
    A) Bandura and Skinner
    B) Zimbardo and Millon
    C) Milgram and Zimbardo
    D) Milgram and Zamboni

94. What do dispositional attributions of behavior entail?
    A) Temperament, luck, and social etiquette
    B) Intelligence, maturity, personality
    C) Interference from others, environment, success
    D) Attitudes, social learning, life experiences

95. The _____ attribution error applies to how we perceive _____ behavior.
    A) Social; our own
    B) Judgment; other people's
    C) Situational; our own
    D) Fundamental; other people's

96. Attitudes influence behavior _____ strongly when situational factors that contradict our attitudes are _____.
    A) More; weak
    B) Less; weak
    C) Less; strong
    D) More; strong

97. The lines experiment by Solomon Asch demonstrated what?
    A) That many people do not pay close attention to their peers
    B) How peer pressure is a powerful motivator
    C) How people will comply with the demands of authority figures
    D) The tendency for research participants to want to please the researcher(s)

98. What is the term used to describe what happens when the average opinion of a group's members tends to become more extreme?
    A) Groupthink
    B) Groupshift
    C) Group polarization
    D) Group dichotomy

99. _____ is behavior aimed at unselfishly helping others and concern for their welfare.
    A) Loyalty
    B) Motivation
    C) Altruism
    D) Good samaritan

100. Which of the following deals with judging another culture solely by the values and standards of one's own culture?
    A) Ethnocentrism
    B) Stereotypes
    C) Race
    D) Prejudice

101. Which of the following refers to a negative attitude towards people of a certain group?
    A) Stereotypes
    B) Ethnocentrism
    C) Discrimination
    D) Prejudice

102. The door-in-the-face technique includes making a small request in order to build the other person up to accepting larger requests.
    A) True
    B) False

103. According to the reciprocity norm, humans are more likely to perform a good deed if _____.
    A) They think it will benefit them later
    B) Someone does something kind for them
    C) They think someone is watching them
    D) A person is clearly in need

104. Conformity is generally strongest in cultures where _____.
    A) Diversity is valued
    B) There is a low incidence of bullying
    C) Collective group identity is stressed
    D) Individualism is valued

105. A student in a classroom who does not raise her hand when the teacher asks a question is exhibiting what kind of behavior?
    A) Social loafing
    B) Groupthink
    C) Ignoring
    D) Social slacking

106. Which of the following is an example of the connection between aggression and self-esteem?
    A) A brain damage victim showing aggressive behavior
    B) A soldier in the army exhibiting aggressive behavior
    C) A person learning aggressive behavior from playing video games
    D) A bully becoming aggressive in response to feeling threatened

107. Which of the following helps to regulate daily biological rhythms?
    A) Epinephrine
    B) Progesterone
    C) Melatonin
    D) Norepinephrine

108. What is the purpose of the control group in a study?
    A) To allow researchers to experiment with different tests
    B) To support the hypothesis
    C) To distinguish between different potential causes
    D) To allow someone in the group to be in charge

109. _____ increases the risk that people will develop distorted memories about events in response to leading questions.
    A) Trauma
    B) Hypnosis
    C) Drug usage
    D) Narcolepsy

110. Stage IV is the lightest form/phase of sleep.
    A) True
    B) False

111. An agonist is a drug that increases the action of a neurotransmitter.
    A) True
    B) False

112. Which Gestalt principle states that humans have a tendency to categorize images into a foreground and background?
    A) Law of proximity
    B) Reciprocity
    C) Law of continuity
    D) Figure-ground relations

113. Olfaction is another name for sense of smell.
    A) True
    B) False

114. _____ is an additional taste sensation that increases the intensity of other taste qualities.
    A) Gustation
    B) Taste receptors
    C) Umami
    D) Umani

115. Which kind of coping method attempts to confront and directly deal with the demands of the situation?
    A) Emotion-focused
    B) Social support seeking
    C) Protective factors
    D) Problem-focused

116. Associative strategies of control involve distracting oneself from the painful sensory input.
    A) True
    B) False

117. According to Bandura, a "live model" of learning involves demonstrating a behavior for someone else.
    A) True
    B) False

118. _____ is used to identify clusters of behaviors that are highly correlated with one another.
    A) An algorithm
    B) Cluster correlational factor
    C) Factor analysis
    D) Faction analysis

119. Which kind of reasoning starts with specific facts to develop a general principle?
    A) Heuristic reasoning
    B) Deductive reasoning
    C) Inductive reasoning
    D) Inclusive reasoning

120. Which of the following is not related to modes of thought?
    A) Motoric thought
    B) Conscious thought
    C) Propositional thought
    D) Imaginal thought

Practice Exam Answer Key

1. B	2. D	3. A
4. C	5. A	6. C
7. A	8. C	9. B
10. D	11. B	12. A
13. C	14. D	15. A
16. B	17. D	18. C
19. D	20. A	21. D
22. B	23. C	24. C
25. A	26. B	27. D
28. D	29. C	30. D
31. B	32. A	33. C
34. B	35. C	36. A
37. A	38. B	39. A
40. D	41. C	42. B
43. B	44. C	45. A
46. C	47. D	48. A
49. C	50. B	51. C
52. A	53. C	54. B
55. B	56. C	57. D
58. A	59. C	60. D
61. C	62. B	63. A
64. C	65. D	66. B

67. D	68. A	69. A
70. B	71. D	72. C
73. C	74. B	75. A
76. D	77. C	78. B
79. A	80. D	81. C
82. D	83. C	84. B
85. A	86. A	87. B
88. C	89. D	90. B
91. C	92. A	93. C
94. B	95. D	96. A
97. B	98. C	99. C
100. A	101. D	102. B
103. B	104. C	105. A
106. D	107. C	108. C
109. B	110. B	111. A
112. D	113. A	114. C
115. D	116. B	117. A
118. C	119. C	120. B

www.ingramcontent.com/pod-product-compliance
Lightning Source LLC
Chambersburg PA
CBHW041528220426
43671CB00002B/19